Thread work Unraveled

Sarah Ann Smith

American Quilter's Society
P. O. Box 3290 • Paducah, KY 42002-3290
www.AmericanQuilter.com

Located in Paducah, Kentucky, the American Quilter's Society (AQS) is dedicated to promoting the accomplishments of today's quilters. Through its publications and events, AQS strives to honor today's quiltmakers and their work and to inspire future creativity and innovation in quiltmaking.

EXECUTIVE BOOK EDITOR: ANDI MILAM REYNOLDS
SENIOR BOOK EDITOR: LINDA BAXTER LASCO
GRAPHIC DESIGN: ELAINE WILSON
COVER DESIGN: MICHAEL BUCKINGHAM
PHOTOGRAPHY: CHARLES R. LYNCH, FINISHED PROJECTS UNLESS OTHERWISE NOTED
STEP-BY-STEP PHOTOGRAPHY: SARAH ANN SMITH

Quotes pages 6, 7 and 65. Reprinted with the permission of Scribner, an imprint of Simon & Schuster Adult Publishing Group, from ON WRITING: A MEMOIR OF THE CRAFT by Stephen King. Copyright ©2000 by Stephen King. All rights reserved.

Quote page 50. Reprinted with the permission of Simon & Schuster Adult Publishing Group, from THE CREATIVE HABIT: Learn It and Use It for Life by Twyla Tharp, Mark Reiter. Copyright ©2003 W.A.T. Ltd.

Attention Photocopying Service: Please note the following—publishers and author give permission to photocopy pages 93–94, 105, and 108 for personal use only.

Additional copies of this book may be ordered from the American Quilter's Society, PO Box 3290, Paducah, KY 42002-3290, or online at www.AmericanQuilter.com.

Library of Congress Cataloging-in-Publication Data

Smith, Sarah Ann, 1957-
Threadwork unraveled / by Sarah Ann Smith.
    p. cm.
ISBN 978-1-57432-999-5
1. Machine quilting. 2. Thread. I. Title.
TT835.S6185 2009
746.46--dc22
                          2009033365

American Quilter's Society
P. O. Box 3290 • Paducah, KY 42002-3290
www.AmericanQuilter.com

Dedication

To
Mother, Joyce,
and the memories of
Daddy, Macho, and Charlie,
who have been there for
as long as I can remember
and to
Paul,
Joshua, and
Eli,
who are my life.

THE WONDER OF THREAD

Fabrics are what have meant color to me—
Thread was just to hold them together
Until I took a close look at what's out there today.
You could have toppled me down with a feather!
There are threads in so many fibers and shades,
Textures and weights also vary you know,
From the finest to thickest, shiny to dull,
They're a real adventure to sew.
So I buy some of this kind, a spool of that,
Letting them all beguile
Then arrange them on racks or lined up in drawers.
Just looking at them makes me smile!
And they add so much dash to my projects,
Giving them a special bloom.
Besides it's a great pleasure to have
Another rainbow in my sewing room!

Jacquie Scuitto, a.k.a. the QuiltMuse
Springfield, Vermont

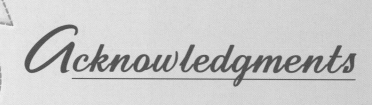

Acknowledgments

Thanks to all who have encouraged me in this quilting journey, including my family, who understand that without my passion I'd go crazier than I already am, and to my friends and students who aid and abet me!

Marie Z. Johansen is one of those best friends in your whole life. Every quilter should be lucky enough to have friends like The Frayed Edges: Hannah Beattie, Deborah Boschert, Kate Cutko, and Kathy Daniels. Thanks also to the Coastal Quilters of Camden, Maine, for letting me test-drive lectures and classes, Marjorie Hallowell, of Maine-ly Sewing (www.mainelysewing.com), who invited me to teach my first classes, and listmom Judy Smith and the members of the www.quiltart.com e-list. Thanks to Iris Karp of Misty Fuse (www.mistyfuse.com), Janome America (www.janome.com), and Hobbs Bonded Fibers (www.hobbsbondedfibers.com) for their support, and my pattern testers.

None of us would be where we are without the example of the masters who came before us. I'm honored and humbled that Hollis Chatelain, Jane Sassaman, and Pamela Allen have lent their works for this book.

Karey Patterson Bresenhan not only supports quilting for the world, her quiet, personal encouragement means so much to me—thank you. Thanks to Pokey Bolton and Cate Prato, (www.quiltingarts.com) for the opportunities they have given me, and to Vicki Anderson and Kit Robinson at Machine Quilting Unlimited (www.mqumag.com) for inviting me to be a columnist. Especially, thanks to the kindly souls at AQS: Meredith Schroeder; my intrepid editor, Linda Lasco, who waded through my verbosity; Andi Reynolds; Elaine Wilson; Michael Buckingham; and Charley Lynch, all of whom turned a rough draft into a book!

No list of thanks is complete without my family. My husband Paul is my best friend, partner, and makes it possible for me to pursue this passion. Our boys, Joshua and Eli, are as essential to life as breathing! My guys make my life complete. Lastly, scritches for the critters, who gleefully shed hair on everything.

Contents

Introduction

I love to quilt. I love to make art. I love color, lots of color! I love to make things with my hands and imagination and sewing machine. Thank you for letting me share these loves with you!

Today's quilters have a wealth of techniques and materials available to them. Using our fabulous sewing machines, their built-in stitches, and free-motion stitching, we can personalize our work with thread. This book will help you learn to use thread on the surface of a quilt, garment, or other project with appliqué, embellishment, and quilting.

Any creative endeavor requires a certain set of skills. In many instances, the skills apply to many different creative activities, while others are specific to what you want to do. And it is easy (Yes, it really is!) to learn those skills, then practice them. Hesiod, an ancient Greek dude wrote (circa 700 B.C.):

The price of achievement is toil, and the gods have ruled you must pay in advance.

In other words: practice! Your reward is mastering the skills and, as a result, having the ability to make what you want.

This book is about:

- ❧ Thread, which is as important as fabric and as much fun to collect
- ❧ Understanding your tools and materials
- ❧ Learning the skills one step at a time
- ❧ Mastering the skills with practice
- ❧ Doing what we love: quilting!

While you set about acquiring the skills and knowledge, have fun while you're doing it and realize that just a bit of magic is happening. Native Mainer and author of a ba-zillion bestsellers, Stephen King, wrote a book titled *On Writing: A Memoir of the Craft,* but his observations can be applied to any creative effort. Where King says "writing," I'll ask you to think "quilting:"

Some of this book—perhaps too much—has been about how I learned to do it. Much of it has been about how you can do it better. The rest of it—and perhaps the best of it—is a permission slip: you can, you should, and if you're brave enough to start, you will. Writing is magic, as much the water of life as any other creative art. The water is free. So drink. Drink and be filled up. (p. 270)

Cheers,
Sarah

The Basics

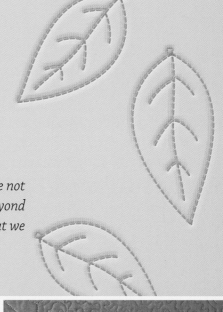

At its most basic we are only discussing a learned skill, but do we not agree that sometimes the most basic skills can create things far beyond our expectations? [As] we move along, you'd do well to remember that we are also talking about magic. (p. 137)

Stephen King wrote this about writing; it applies equally to quilting.

When he was a boy, King helped his Uncle Oren make a repair on the house. They toted an old, large, heavy toolbox, but in the end, only used eight screws and a screwdriver. When Stephen asked why they had brought the whole heavy box, his uncle replied:

I didn't know what else I might find to do once I got out here, did I? It's best to have your tools with you. If you don't, you're apt to find something you didn't expect and get discouraged.

Quilters and other artists need to build their own toolboxes, too. This first section talks about the tools and materials you use to make things—the basics. It will help you get good results. Without the basics, you may end up with a colorful item in the waste bin or UFO (UnFinished Object) pile!

If you have ever painted a house, you know that proper preparation is key. The same thing applies to machine sewing, decorative stitching, and quilting. Just like sanding the windowsill before you paint, you want to prepare your fabric, your machine, and your workspace for machine work.

I'd like for you not just to learn what the "rules" are, but why they are, and what the repercussions are if you break the rules. Then, if you need to break them to get the look you want, you'll be able to counteract or minimize any unwanted side effects. This applies to your design decisions as well as techniques, but for now, let's concentrate on the basics of construction and technique.

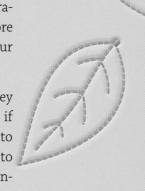

Thread

Thread is as important a choice as fabric, and it's a whole new thing to collect! The artist in traditional art media uses a wide selection of paints...and **you** need a wide selection of colors in thread so your quilt will look and last the way you want. Here's my first true confession of the book: I not only have one of each color in regular 50-wt. sewing cotton but also in 60-wt. cotton, and I'm working on finishing out a full range of 40- and 60-wt. polyesters, *and* I have a growing collection of metallics and specialty threads.

Consider the use *and* the appearance of the thread. Are you going to piece, appliqué, embroider/embellish, couch, and/or quilt? You also need to consider the purpose of the quilt. Will it be a wall quilt or a well-used, often-washed lap or bed quilt? I have such a wide range of thread types and fibers because I need the right tool for the job.

Thread Weight and Plies

First, let's look at weights of thread. Thread is made of several plies, or strands, of thread twisted together. Often you will find a measurement on the end of a spool that looks like this: 50/3. The first number is a measurement of the thread; the second is the number of plies or strands in the thread. A medium-weight piecing thread labeled #50 means that 50 kilometers of that thread weighs one kilogram. A 60/2 cotton thread is made of two plies of #60 thread and is a bit finer.

Since I can never remember that definition,

I think of it as similar to the thread-count in sheets. The higher the number, the more of that thread it takes to fill up an inch. For example, a 350-count sheet will be woven from finer threads of cotton than a 100-count sheet, just as it would take more 100-wt. silk to fill a given space than a heavy 35-wt. machine quilting cotton.

Most quilters use a 50/3 or 50/2 cotton thread for machine and hand piecing. It is strong, yet not too thick. A 60/2 thread makes a great hand or machine appliqué thread. Since it is finer, it tends to "disappear" into the appliqué. However, if your quilt is destined for a child's bed, you may opt to use a heavier (and a bit more visible) and more durable thread so that it will stand up to the wear and tear of fort-building and extra washing it will get.

Similarly, you may find that a fine or medium-heavy polyester thread may give the look and durability you prefer (samples 3 and 4 in the photo right).

If you want to make an heirloom quilt that will receive special handling, you might choose very fine 100-wt. silk. Or you might choose to use a clear or smoke-colored monofilament thread. Only you can decide on the look you want for your quilt.

When it comes time to actually choose a thread, use two simple tests:

For strength, grab the thread between your hands and try to break it. If you need your thread to be strong (remember the kids' quilts?) and the thread you have selected breaks easily, you may want to pick a different thread!

For appearance, just look at the thread. Even if the labels say your possible selections are all the same weight, if one looks thicker than the others, trust what you see.

Here's a mantra to internalize and live by:

Make visual decisions visually.

The thread industry recently established a new measurement to be consistent among all manufacturers and all fibers called "tex." Tex is the weight in grams of 9000 meters of thread. A very fine silk thread might weigh tex 10, a very heavy topstitching thread could be tex 68, while a medium-weight piecing thread might be tex 20. The tex system was developed because a cotton labeled 60-wt. may very well not be the same thickness as a polyester labeled 60-wt.

How Is Thread Made?

What goes into making thread? I went straight to the source of great knowledge, Bob Purcell, co-owner with his wife, Heather, of Superior Threads (www.superiorthreads.com).

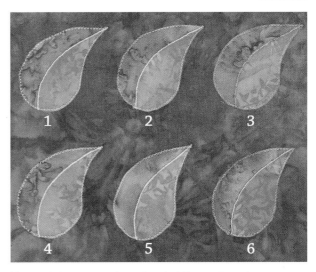

Identical shapes appliquéd with different threads

QUESTION: I know cotton thread starts with cotton bolls from the plant that are spun and dyed, but there has to be more to it than that. How is cotton thread made?

ANSWER: The cotton fiber is first separated from the cotton seed. The fiber is then dried to reduce moisture and improve the fiber quality. It is cleaned to remove leaf trash, sticks, and other foreign matter. The raw fiber, called lint, is compressed into bales, sampled for classification, wrapped, and shipped to textile mills.

The mills produce cotton yarn and cloth by first carding the cotton. Carding is the process of pulling the fibers into parallel alignment to form a thin web. The web is then combed, which removes impurities and makes the fibers smoother. The final step is spinning the fibers to make uniform strands.

Further processing may be done to make a mercerized, glazed, or gassed thread.

Mercerizing is a process of treating cotton thread with an alkali solution, causing the fibers to swell. This process allows the dye to better penetrate the fibers, thereby increasing the luster. Mercerizing increases the strength of the thread and reduces the amount of lint.

Dyeing thread at a factory in Japan

Gassing, the technical term for "silk finish" or "polished cotton," refers to passing a cotton thread through a flame at high speed, burning off the excess fuzz in order to create a higher sheen.

The strength and quality of cotton thread is often measured by the length of the staple. Egyptian long staple cottons are 1.25" long. Egyptian extra-long staples are a minimum of 1.37" long.

The higher the quality of the thread, the less special handling will be required. Poor quality thread has much lint and breaks easily and can take the joy out of any sewing project. Each type of thread has specific characteristics and will behave

Glazing involves heating the thread and then coating it with waxes, starches, and other chemicals. The thread is then polished to a high luster. Glazing results in a glossy thread with a hard finish. Glazed thread is usually stiffer than unglazed thread. Most professionals do not recommend glazed threads for machine work because the glaze rubs off and gums up the machine.

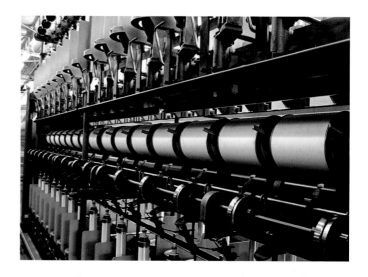

Thread being wound onto the spool

differently in sewing machines. Threads are either made of a natural fiber—cotton, wool, silk, linen—or synthetic fibers—rayon, polyester, nylon).

What About Thread Types?

QUESTION: Where do polyester threads come from? Are they spun and plied like cotton, extruded, or how? What about metallics and holographic threads? How are they different in their manufacture from "regular" cotton and polyester sewing threads? And what about monofilament?

ANSWER: There are many types of thread based on different thread construction methods and fiber content:

Spun thread: Cotton or polyester staple fibers are spun into single yarns and then twisted together.

Core thread: Spun cotton or polyester staple fibers are wrapped around polyester fibers.

Textured thread: Polyester or nylon is mechanically textured to make the thread fuzzy and stretchy and woolly-like. Texturing is a procedure used to increase the volume and the elasticity of a filament yarn. The essential properties of textured yarns and the products made from them are softness, fullness, a high degree of elasticity, thermal insulation, and moisture-transporting properties.

Filament Round: This shiny thread is made of strands of polyester, rayon, or nylon.

Monofilament: A single nylon or polyester filament. Polyester is preferred.

Beyond cotton, a variety of fibers is used in thread.

Fiber Content	Manufacturing Process	Advantages	Disadvantages
Rayon	produced by pressing cellulose acetate through small holes and solidifying it in the form of filaments	* high sheen * soft * relatively heat resistant	* not colorfast * not as strong as polyester * less durable than polyester
Polyester	3 types synthetically produced from polymer resins: * spun poly: fiber staples spun together; looks like cotton * filament poly: continuous fiber * trilobal poly: a higher quality polyester with a sheen equal to rayon or silk; lint free	* durable; designed for heavy duty use * strong with more tensile strength than rayon or cotton * colorfast * shape retention * stretch recovery * can be made with a matte or high sheen finish	* low melting temperature
Nylon	synthetic thread occasionally used in the form of a monofilament clear or textured, fuzzy (woolly-like) thread	* strength	* low melting temperature * not colorfast * becomes brittle through laundering and exposure The negatives far outweigh the positives; use with caution.

Major thanks to Bob for this information. The Education tab at www.superiorthreads.com is a wonderful resource!

Selecting Threads

In most garment making and quilt piecing, we use the same weight and color of thread in the bobbin as through the needle. But guess what: you don't have to! You can and sometimes should use a different weight thread in the bobbin than you use in the needle. And you don't have to use just one thread at a time! (I'll warn you now: I have ideas...lots of them!) It is possible to thread two threads through one needle, stitching as if the two threads were two plies of a single thread. This is tons of fun when embellishing and embroidering, making thread lace, and even when quilting.

Bobbin threads come in a wide array of colors. The advantage of these fine threads (usually 60-wt) is that you can get many more inches of thread on each bobbin than you could of a 50-wt or even a 60-wt cotton. I use a fine polyester bobbin thread for virtually all my appliqué and most of my quilting.

Today, we are blessed with (and sometimes confused by) a dizzying array of choices. You can even have a rainbow on one spool of thread. Using variegated threads can add unexpected life and zing to your quilt, but can also pose a challenge in picking a color that doesn't fade in and jump out across the surface (unless, of course, that is what you want it to do). You can combine threads and colors to customize the look of your project.

The thread tension sampler (page 13) teaches how best to do test-runs on pairing threads and setting a balanced tension. And on page 64 you'll find a stitch-out sampler comparing several quilting patterns repeated in different fibers and weights of threads.

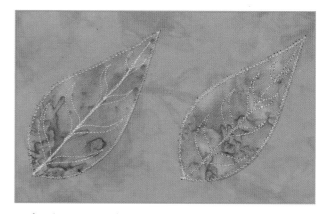

Leaf with one color for veining and another with plied threads

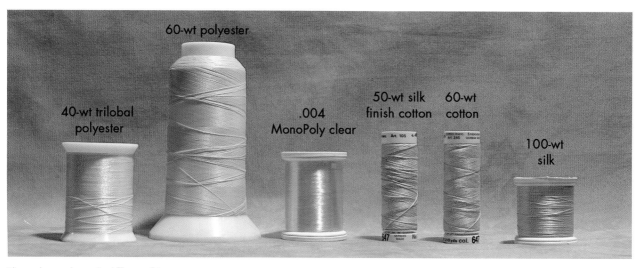

Threads made with different fibers

Thread Tension Sampler

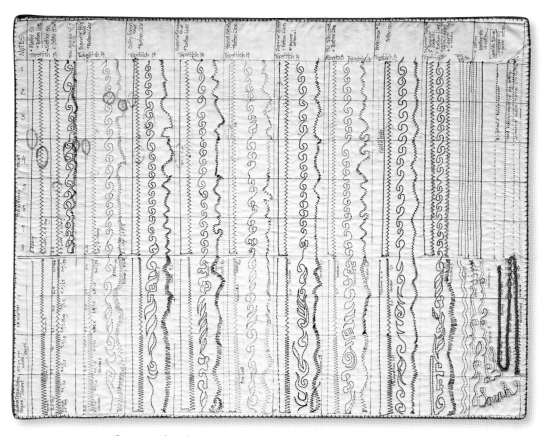

Now that you've learned a bit about thread, I'd like to show you how to make a Thread Tension Quick-Reference Sampler.

Fabrics and Notions

- 16" x 21" light, plain fabric for the top *(Muslin is perfect.)*
- 20" x 25" light, plain fabric for the backing
- 20" x 25" batting
- Black or blue fine-tip permanent fabric marking pen such as a Pigma® Micron® marker
- Colored fabric marking pen
- Assorted sewing machine needles suitable to the threads you select *(I used Quilting sizes 11/75 and 14/90, Topstitch 14/90, and Denim 14/90. You may prefer a smaller size, perhaps a 12.)*
- Assorted threads, including 50-wt. cotton; clear monofilament; variegated (cotton, rayon and/or polyester); trilobal polyester (the shiny kind); rayon, metallics, and holographic threads

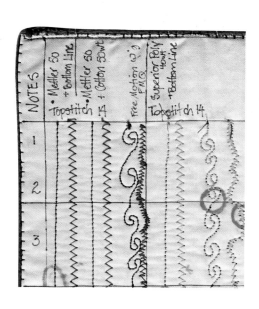

Part One—The Upper Table

Mark a grid on your top fabric using the black fabric marker. Start ½" from the edge, marking horizontal lines 1½" apart, vertical lines 2" apart.

Label the upper left box "Thread/Needle Info." Add numbers down the first column.

Make a quilt sandwich with your gridded top, batting, and backing.

Use HIGHLY contrasting threads, with a different color in the top and bobbin. This combination allows you to easily see which thread is doing what.

You don't have to sew the whole chart in one sitting (Can you say tedious?), but every time you have a new thread and needle combination, sew another column for future reference.

Install a walking foot on your machine. Start with your favorite "basic" combination, probably a 50-wt. cotton thread in both the needle and bobbin and a sharp needle (perhaps a Quilting size 11/75). For each thread and needle combination, select a straight stitch, length 2.5. Set your needle tension to "1" and sew down through box 1. When you reach the line to box 2, raise the needle tension to "2." Repeat this process, through your highest tension.

In the top row of your grid, note the top thread brand, weight, and fiber content, bobbin thread (ditto), and needle type of your thread and needle combinations. For example, my favorites include Yenmet Metallic, Glitter by Superior Threads, two-threads-handled-as-one, and twin needle stitching.

Repeat with the same thread and needle combination using a zigzag stitch. Then switch to a free-motion foot and try free-motion straight line and zigzag stitching, changing the thread tension at each new box.

As you complete each row of stitching, look at the front to see where the bobbin thread begins to show, mark that with your fingers, then flip it over and check the back for where the needle thread begins to show. The "sweet spot" is where the two threads best balance/meet in the center of the quilt sandwich the best.

Use a fabric marker on the sampler to indicate the best setting. The "perfect" tension varies greatly depending on which threads and needle you use and whether you're using the walking foot or quilting free motion. Each machine is individual; it is likely that your settings will vary from that of a friend doing the same sampler, even if she has the same make and model machine as you.

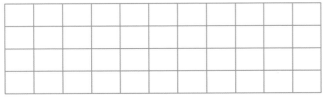

Sample of a Thread Tension quick-reference chart

Part Two—The Lower Table

Once you have established the best tension setting for a given combination, set your machine to that setting. Then try varying the length and/or width of the stitch. Each time you cross a grid line, change the length of the stitch and mark the stitch length in each grid. Using different stitch lengths will change the appearance of the threads, especially the shiny ones, which reflect even more light with slightly longer stitch lengths. If you want to "tone down the glitz," a shorter stitch length will do that by casting more shadows.

You may find that as you start quilting with a more natural speed and rhythm (as opposed to stopping and starting every two inches) you need to adjust your "perfect" tension slightly. Check the thread balance the same way as before. If you need to alter the tension, do so and make a note of the "new perfect tension" at the top of the sampler.

Now you have a ready-reference chart, customized to your machine and favorite thread combinations. When you begin to quilt a new project, prepare a test sandwich using leftover bits of your top, batting, and backing fabric to fine tune tension settings. With the sampler, you have a jump-start on the process because you can check it first to see where to start.

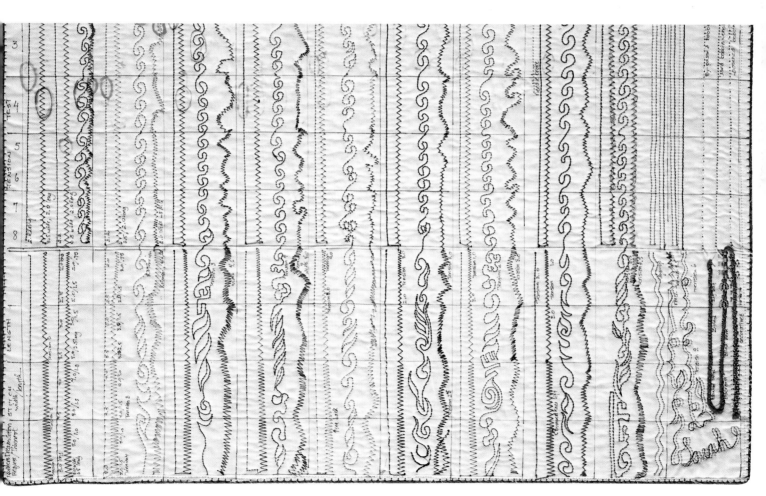

Sampler detail

Needles

Needle Sizes

There are almost as many types of needles as there are fabrics and threads, and for good reason. Each is specialized to do a specific job well. You want to select a needle that is compatible with both your materials (thread and fabric) and the technique you're using (piecing, appliqué, embroidery, or quilting).

Think of it this way: you wouldn't wear high heels to go hiking on a rocky trail, and most folks wouldn't wear hiking boots to a formal wedding.

Back in the dark ages of my childhood, in the 60s, we used Universal needles, which are halfway between a Ballpoint and a Sharp. They worked well with the poly-cotton blend threads and fabrics of the era, but they don't work as well as other needles for what we do today with decorative stitching and quilting.

Needles for home sewing machines range in size from 60–120 (European) and 8–19 (US). Packages are usually labeled with both sizes. For example, my favorite Topstitch needles are size 90/14. The larger the number, the thicker the needle. Needles are made of wire. Some, such as Denims, are made of a more rigid metal so they can better pierce heavier fabrics.

A smaller needle will make a smaller hole in your fabric. If you are using a very fine fabric, such as a lightweight china silk or cotton lawn, you will want to select a small needle such as a Microtex or Sharp 60/8. If your project includes heavy upholstery fabrics or canvas, or has a lot of layers of fused cloth, you will want at least a size 14 needle. Most piecing is done with a size 10, 11, or 12 sharp-pointed needle.

If you are sewing on cloth that has been painted, you may wish to select a smaller size than you might otherwise (and risk a bit of fraying or breakage of the thread), since the paint on the cloth will not allow the weave of the cloth to snug up at the hole. The smaller needle size will minimize the appearance of the hole.

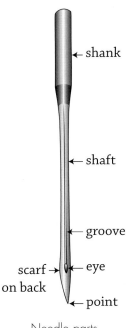

shank

shaft

groove

scarf → eye
on back

point

Needle parts

Anatomy of a Needle

The **shank** is the portion of the needle that slides up into the needle shaft on your sewing machine.

The thread snuggles into the **groove** that runs down the front of the needle, which protects the thread from friction and abrasion. The **eye** of the needle is the hole the thread passes through. Think of *The Three Bears*: you want the Baby Bear needle for your thread—not too big, not too small, but "just right."

Select a needle whose groove and eye match the weight and type of thread you will be using. If the groove and eye are too large, the thread will flop around and form a sloppy-looking stitch. If the groove and eye are too small, the thread will sit on the outside of the needle and become frayed as you stitch and break. Some manufacturers have begun recommending needle types and sizes best suited to their threads.

Marginalia: Did you know that in a straight stitch, at a stitch length of 2.5, it takes 14–17 stitches from the first time the thread passes through the fabric until it is finally sewn onto the fabric? If your thread isn't fully protected in the groove, it will fray a little bit with each stitch!

The **scarf** is the "scoop-y out-y place" on the back of the needle. As the needle descends to the lowest point in the bobbin area, the hook of the bobbin travels around the needle at the scarf area. The needle and bobbin threads lock together and form a stitch. If your needle isn't inserted into the shaft properly, the bobbin hook can't do its job.

If your machine is "out of timing" it means the hook and the scarf don't meet the way they are supposed to but rub (not good) or jam (worse). If you manage to knock the machine out of timing by slamming a needle into the throat plate (eeek, ooops, shriek!), the needle will not be at the fully down position when the bobbin hook passes the needle. This is not a good thing and usually requires an expensive trip to the sewing machine doctor.

The **point** of the needle pierces the fabric. Different types of needles have different points, from Ballpoint (rounded), to Universal (between rounded and sharp), to Sharp, which is the best for threadwork.

Needle Types

A broad range of needle types come in assorted sizes. Slight variations in the shape of the eye, the point, the shape of the scarf, the depth of the groove, and the strength/flexibility of the metal in the needle make a difference in how well each performs a given task with a given thread.

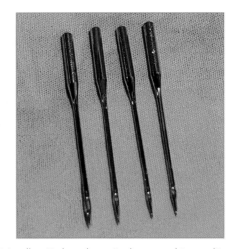

Metallic, Embroidery, Quilting, and Jeans/Denim

> **Tip**
>
> To make sure the needle is inserted all the way into the shaft, stick a straight pin into the eye of the needle and gently push up on the needle to hold it in place while you tighten the needle screw.

- **Sharp**—for piecing, some quilting
- **Denim or Jeans/Denim**—for work on heavy fabrics like denim, upholstery fabrics, densely fused pieces, and some quilting
- **Quilting**—for quilting with cotton quilting threads
- **Leather**—for sewing on real and artificial leather, and real and synthetic suede fabrics
- **Microtex**—for sewing on microfiber and other fine, densely woven fabrics such as blouse-weight fabrics and silks
- **Metallic or Metafil**—for machine embroidery or quilting with metallic threads
- **Embroidery**—for less friction and breakage of heavier and textured threads; has a larger eye than most needles; good for some quilting
- **Topstitch**—for decorative threads; the deeper groove provides more protection for the thread; it has the largest eye of any sewing machine needle; good for quilting as well as decorative stitching (feed dogs up or free motion)
- **Universal**—Jack of all trades, master of none
- **Stretch**—for stretch fabrics used in exercise and swim wear
- **Ballpoint**—for knit fabrics such as tee-shirt jersey
- **Twin, Triple, Wing**—for specialized and heirloom sewing

Marginalia: Some threads require a very large eye to prevent fraying and breakage. Because I use 40-wt. trilobal polyester threads for much of my quilting, I use the Topstitch 90/14 recommended by the thread manufacturer.

The size and shape of the **eye** affect how the thread passes through the needle. In the photo above, you can see that the eye of the Topstitch needle is nearly double the size of the eye of the

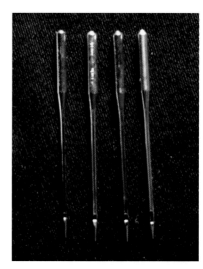

The eye of the Topstitch needle on the right is nearly twice as large as the eyes in the quilting, jeans/denim, and embroidery needles on the left.

Quilting and Denim needles of the same size. Notice that the top of the Topstitch eye is more flat and less rounded. If you are using a holographic thread (the kind that looks a thin ribbon of Mylar), the flat edge passes through the Topstitch eye more smoothly and with fewer attitudinous moments.

You can make perfectly parallel lines by using a Twin needle. You can use the same color thread in each needle or two different colors to create a calligraphic effect. These needles are expensive, so it is a good idea to stitch slowly and carefully. Many newer sewing machines have a setting so that you can't select a stitch that would cause a Twin needle to slam into the throat plate. Check your sewing machine owner's manual for more information.

THE SPECIAL CASE OF METALLIC THREADS

Metallic or Metafil needles have a large eye, but for me, most metallic threads perform better and break less when I use a Topstitch or Embroidery needle instead. Try the different types and see which works best for you.

When using metallic and other "crunchy" threads in the needle, use a very smooth, fine thread in the bobbin. A cotton thread in the bobbin, no matter how fine, smooth, and beautifully manufactured, will have small slubs or little fibers that snag and grab onto metallic threads. Using a fine, smooth polyester such as The Bottom Line™ by Superior or a rayon thread will permit the needle and bobbin threads to loop around each other and play nicely together. Monofilament in the bobbin can also be used successfully.

Remember that metallic thread is partly metal, the needle is all metal, and metal conducts heat! If you have been merrily quilting away for an hour or so with a seemingly perfect combination of needle, metallic, and bobbin thread, and all of a sudden you start having problems, simply swap out the needle in the machine for a cool, fresh needle. You don't need to throw out the one you've been using. Just pop it in a pincushion or needle-keeper and let it cool off. When you resume with a cool needle, the chances are high that your problems will be solved (and if they're not, rethread your machine!).

When to Change Needles

Because we are asking needles to do things other than stitch together two layers of cloth when we machine appliqué, embroider, or quilt, needles get worn out and dull more quickly than when piecing quilt tops or constructing garments.

Some sources say you should change needles every 8–12 hours of stitching, but I never have a clue how many hours of actual sewing I do on a given project. Other sources say change needles every two-to-three bobbins used completely. Yet others recommend a new needle for every project. Are you as confused as I was?

METALLIC THREADS & STENCILED LEAVES, detail showing metallic thread

First, listen to the sound of a nice, new, sharp needle. Then listen to a needle that you have used for paper-piecing or quilting for *many* hours. The used needle will make a "thunk" or dull popping sound. When your needle starts making that sound, it is time to change needles.

Second, if the "ick" moment has happened and you have managed to bang the needle into the throat plate (and it didn't break), change the needle as soon as possible.

Third, if a needle lasts through an entire project, it probably needs changing, even if the project is relatively small. It is the number of stitches a needle makes, not the overall size of the project, that matters.

If you're still not sure, run your fingernail (carefully) down the shaft of the needle. If you feel even a tiny snag, rough, or dull spot, change the needle.

Finally, if you can't remember the last time you changed your needle (and you know who you are), it is time to change the needle!

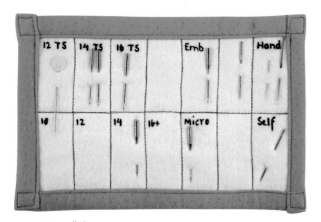

Needlekeeper, pattern on page 22

Troubleshooting

If you're not getting good stitches:

- Rethread both the needle and the bobbin.
- Try changing the needle; even if it is brand new out of the package, it is possible it isn't sharp.
- Try a different type of needle, even one that isn't "supposed" to work. Try the least obvious choice, then try what you have on hand, one at a time, until something does work.
- Take a walk! Sometimes just getting away makes things better.

How to Remember Which Needle Is in Your Machine

There are handy little doo-hickies (a technical term) that stick onto your machine and allow you to slide markers to the size and type of needle currently in use. The drawback is that you must remember to move the markers. Ahem.

Be consistent in where you keep your needle cases. I keep new needles in a drawer by my machine. I keep "in use" packs of needles to the right of the machine. I pick the needle on the far right of the package first; if it still has more miles to go before being recycled, I return it to that spot. When I have tossed that one as dull, I use the next needle, but return it to the far-right slot. I then know the needle in the far right has been used, but is still good. This is one of the few times in my life that I am methodical!

Make a flat needlekeeper to put under the presser foot when you are not sewing.

Use a tomato or Dresden Plate pincushion. Mark each segment to correspond with the needles you prefer. I fused small bits of lime green onto my Dresden Plate pincushion for labels. Find a way-funky hat pin so that when you remove a needle from a section, you can insert the pin there to let you know that's the one in the machine.

RIGHT: My friend Deborah Boschert made the cute pins using shrink plastic and plain metal straight pins…fun!

Needle Trash Project

Needle Safety

Be kind to critters at the landfills and folks who work with trash and make a needle disposal container. Remove the lid from a plastic film canister or pill bottle. Hold a fat nail with a pair of pliers and heat the tip in a flame (do this near a sink or bowl of water just in case), then melt a hole in the center of the lid. Replace the lid. When you break a needle or swap it out for a new one, slip the old needle in the hole. When the container is full, trade lids with a new canister/pill bottle, tape it shut, and reuse the lid-with-hole on a new bottom.

Needlekeeper Pattern

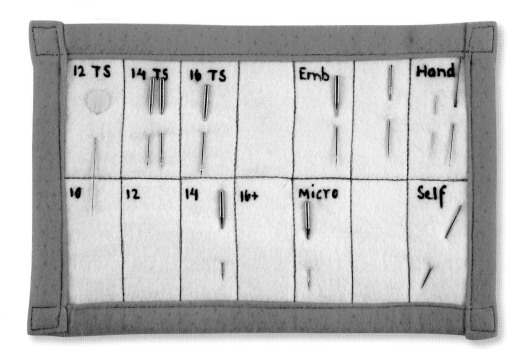

Fabric and Notions

- 5" x 7" flannel or needle-punched batting
- 7" x 9" light color backing
- Fabric marking pen, such as a Pigma Micron
- Flower head or decorative pin

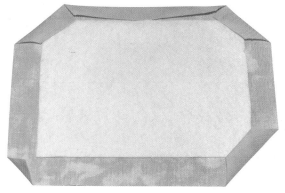

Fold in the sides of the backing

Making the Needlekeeper

Mark the flannel with a horizontal center line and vertical lines 1" apart.

Center the flannel on the backing.

Fold in the sides of the backing to "kiss" the sides of the flannel.

Fold the sides again to overlap the edges of the flannel.

Repeat for the top and bottom edges.

Topstitch the folded backing in place.

Sew the flannel along the marked horizontal and vertical lines.

Label the sections with the types and sizes of the needles you use most.

Use a decorative pin to indicate which needle you have in your machine.

Your Sewing Machine

Useful Features

Many of us are fortunate to own our dream machine, but not everyone is. I'd like to teach you how to do your best job using the machine you have. It always helps to know how to use features you already have and what features are useful when selecting (or dreaming about) a new machine. Here's my list of "really useful" features, why they're so useful, and possible "fixes" if your machine doesn't have a particular feature.

NEEDLE UP, NEEDLE DOWN

When doing *any* free-motion work or satin stitching, I always set my machine to needle-down, which helps prevent unsightly "jogs" in the stitching line. If your machine doesn't have this feature, stop stitching while both hands are on the fabric. Remove your right hand *only*, turn the flywheel towards yourself until the needle is in the fully down position, then re-position your hands and resume sewing.

STITCHES THAT ADJUST LENGTH AND WIDTH IN SMALL INCREMENTS

This feature is especially important in zigzag, blind hem, and blanket stitching. If you want unobtrusive stitches, you need to be able to set the length and width to a size that is small enough to "disappear" visually but still be large enough to bite into the fabric. For example, on my machine, I can adjust my zigzag stitches from 0.0 to 5.0 mm in length. The width increases from 0.0 to 7.0 in .10 increments, which allows me to smoothly taper my satin stitching as I'm sewing. If the increments are larger, for example .5 or 1.0, you'll have visible jogs in your satin stitch.

ADJUSTABLE NEEDLE THREAD TENSION

Many of the new machines have automatic tension for the needle thread. These settings are generally for sewing fabric to fabric, not quilting, free-motion embroidery, or some of the other unusual things we ask our machines to do. If you have automatic tension and it always works perfectly, fantastic! But it is essential to be able to adjust the needle thread tension if needed. If a machine has automatic tension, be sure there is an override function.

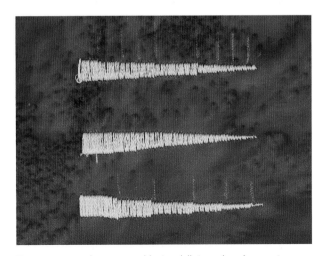

Zigzag taper done smoothly (middle) and with jogs (top and bottom)

LARGER HARP AREA

The harp is the area of your machine between the needle area and the machine housing on the right. One of the hardest parts of machine quilting on a domestic/home machine is fitting the fabric bulk through the harp. With a larger harp, it's less cramped and you can maneuver a bulky project more easily.

SPEED CONTROL (OR HOW TO GET IT IF YOU DON'T HAVE IT ON YOUR MACHINE)

Especially when you are learning free-motion work, doing fussy stitching, or using a heat-sensitive thread like a metallic or holographic, you may want to sew more slowly. By reducing the top speed of your machine, you can "floor it" (press all the way down on the foot pedal) and still not be going too fast to control what you are doing. As well, for free-motion work, it frees you up to concentrate on just one thing: what your hands are doing, without having to coordinate the speed of the needle (via your foot pedal) at the same time.

If you don't have speed control on your machine, tape a bottle cap or small block of wood to your foot pedal so that it doesn't depress all the way when you step on it. That means your maximum speed is slower, which will make it easier

for you to learn free-motion stitching; you won't be scared by the speed. You'll need to take the cap on and off, but it's better than not having a speed control at all, especially when you are learning.

GOOD LIGHTING

Look for a machine that doesn't throw shadows with the presser foot. A light under the harp area is really nice. My eyesight is poor, so I use two lights in addition to the ambient light in the room. I set a flip-up light in front of my machine to cast more light on the area just in front of the needle and use a clip-on-the-desk or floor lamp behind to illuminate from the back.

VISIBILITY AROUND THE PRESSER FOOT AREA

When you are doing free-motion work, you need to see what is behind and to the sides of your needle. Less "stuff" cluttering up your view to the rear makes it much easier to see where you are going when you are moving your project from back to front and side to side.

EASY-TO-SWITCH PRESSER FEET

A walking foot can be awkward to install. An easy mechanism to swap out feet or a built-in dual feed will encourage you to use those features instead of "making do" with a regular presser foot.

FREE-MOTION, QUILTING, OR DARNING FOOT

Depending on your machine's age and brand, the name may vary but these feet are all a variation on the same theme: a foot that either rides above the fabric (a, c, d, e) or hops up when the needle is up and presses down on the fabric as the needle goes down (b). These feet come in clear plastic (a, b) and metal (c, d, e). I prefer a metal one because I think it provides better visibility.

I prefer a *round* free-motion foot (c). If I want to echo quilt—that is, quilt an even distance around something (think of a pebble dropped in a pond)—it is easily done when the foot is the same distance from the needle all the way around.

The open-toe foot (e) provides greater visibility but can snag on embellishments, fused edges, and lumpy seams. A closed-toe foot (c) will glide over things more easily, but doesn't provide the same visibility. I want one of each!

Various free-motion feet

STRAIGHT STITCH VERSUS ZIGZAG THROAT PLATE

The reason the beloved Singer Featherweight makes such a perfect straight stitch is because that is all it does, and it does it with a straight-stitch throat plate—one with a small round hole. Our new machines let us do wonderful decorative stitches, but you need the wider opening in the throat plate to do so. Sometimes the fabric can get pushed down into this larger hole during stitching. A straight stitch throat plate may improve the look of straight stitches, both with the feed dogs up and when doing free-motion stitching. You *must* remember, however, not to switch to zigzag while the straight stitch plate is in place or you'll break a needle and possibly damage your machine.

Marginalia: Use a sticky-note or tape a piece of paper over the stitch width button as a reminder to yourself not to use anything other than a straight stitch until you have changed back to the regular zigzag throat plate.

ADJUSTABLE PRESSER FOOT PRESSURE

Not all fabrics or quilt sandwiches are the same thickness. Sometimes you need to reduce the pressure on the presser foot so that the project feeds through more easily. If you are working with layers of sheers, you may need to increase the pressure to properly feed the fabrics through the machine.

a   b   c   d   e

LOW BOBBIN INDICATOR

Nothing is more annoying than finishing up a long run of quilting only to discover your bobbin thread ran out four feet ago. A light or sound that lets you know you're about to run out is a great feature. Some machines with drop-in bobbins don't have these warnings—they figure you can see the bobbin. Not if you have a big quilt covering it (grumble).

EASILY REMOVED THROAT PLATE

As with any machine, good maintenance habits are a must. A throat plate that is easy to remove will make it easier for you to be diligent about cleaning out accumulated lint. Skipped stitches are often the result of lint in the bobbin area. If your needle is dull, you can actually push little motes of batting into the bobbin area with every stitch. If you are working on fuzzy fabric like flannel or fleece, you need to clean even more frequently.

Check your manual for instructions on oiling: every machine is different. Be sure to use the recommended sewing machine oil—it IS different than other types of machine oil.

The bottom line? There is no perfect machine. Each of us has different needs and desires. Make a list of the features *you* find most essential. When shopping for a new machine, take that list with you, along with your favorite threads, fabrics, and a couple of mini-quilt sandwiches. Test drive various machines using the thread and fabric you like best, and see which machine best suits your needs—not mine, not your best friend's or teacher's, but *yours!*

Thread Matters
YOUR MACHINE'S THREAD PATH

In principle, you want to use a stacked thread on a vertical spindle because on most machines the first step in the thread path is to the side of a vertical spindle. On a machine with an antenna, you may opt to bypass the antenna so the thread feeds off in the correct manner, especially if you're having trouble.

Cross-wound threads can be used on horizontal spindles on most home machines, on vertical spindles that feed up into an antenna, or on thread stands where the spool stands on end.

Why does the feed direction matter? If the thread comes off the spool in the "not intended" way, you will introduce a twist into the thread. Many machines can handle thread coming off the spool either way and some threads, like cotton, are more forgiving. But monofilament, metallic, and holographic threads are frequently less tolerant and will eventually snap and break.

Thread is wound onto spools in one of two ways: cross-wound (3 spools on the left) and stacked (2 spools on the right). Cross-wound thread makes an "X" pattern on the spool and is intended to come off the top when the spool is standing on its end. Stacked thread looks like the edges of a book and is meant to come off the side of the spool when the spool is standing on its end.

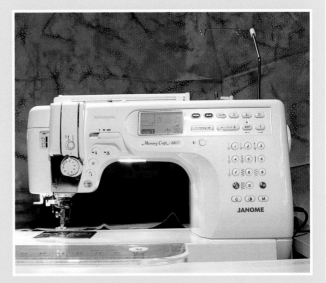

Sewing machines feed thread into the thread path in one of three ways: from a vertical spindle, from a vertical spindle to an "antenna," or from a horizontal spindle. Some machines offer alternate spindles so you can position spools either horizontally or vertically.

USING A THREAD STAND

So what do you do if your machine doesn't have a spindle that accommodates the thread you want to use? Or what if you have both vertical and horizontal spindles but the tension still isn't quite right? Use a thread stand!

Now, I can hear you saying, "But my thread has been the other ("wrong?") way and I've never had any trouble." Fantastic! If your way breaks the "rules" instead of the thread, so be it! BUT, if you've had trouble with thread breakage, try switching the spindle position.

There are two basic types of thread stands, plus adaptors. Inexpensive stands are designed for using cones of threads on home machines (green base). Slightly more expensive ones can accommodate spools standing vertically or horizontally before the thread goes up to the antenna (tan base). There are also adaptors that slide onto a vertical spindle to convert it to horizontal.

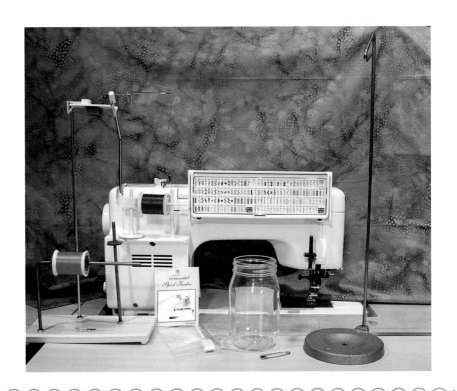

Thread Stand Middle-of-the-Night Fix

So you've decided you need a thread stand, but it's way after store closing hours, or no one near you carries them, or you're at a quilt retreat and your stand is at home. Improvise! Set a jam jar or tall glass behind your sewing machine—one that will hold your spool in the proper orientation. If you need the spool to stand upright, make sure the jar is narrow enough so the spool won't tip over. Tape a large safety pin to the back of your machine near the first step in your thread path with the round loop end up. The loop in the safety pin will be the first step in your improvised thread path. I've seen stands made from wire coat hangers. Get creative!

Thread Tension

Are you afraid to touch your tension dial? Have you ever found that your tension was off but weren't sure how to fix it? If so, I'll help you understand how tension works, how to thread the needle thread path correctly, and how to wind the bobbin correctly. Making the tension sampler (page 13) will help you better understand your machine and how to get the results you want.

First, let me just say that if the manufacturers didn't want us to touch the thread tension, they wouldn't have designed sewing machines with the tension dial smack dab on the front of the machine! The sewing machine companies know that different combinations of thread, fabric, and sometimes batting will often require adjustments to get a balanced tension.

If you're having tension problems, the first thing to check is how your machine is threaded. The Tension Balance figure (page 29) shows properly balanced tension and the two basic problems—the tension on the top is too tight or the tension on the bottom is too tight.

Please READ your sewing machine manual! (I know...a radical concept!) Learn how to adjust the tension (or override automatic tension) on your machine. A higher number on the needle tension dial means tighter tension; a lower number means looser tension.

Think of tension as a tug of war between the elf holding the needle thread and the elf holding the bobbin thread. When the needle carries the top thread down into the bobbin area, the hook on the bobbin passes through the loop created by the needle thread and wraps around it, forming the stitch. Ideally, when your sewing machine completes a stitch, the needle and bobbin threads should cross each other exactly in the middle of the fabric pieces or the quilt sandwich—in other words, the elves are evenly matched in strength.

Then there is the real world. At least ninety percent of all tension issues can be solved by adjusting the needle thread tension. Sometimes, the bobbin thread will pop up to the top. In the tug of war, the needle elf is stronger, pulling the bobbin thread to the top. You need to loosen the top tension.

When the needle thread shows through on the bottom side, your bobbin elf is winning. You need to tighten the top tension. Even when you have set the perfect tension, variations in the movement and speed of your hands and the needle as you free-motion stitch can change the tension in a particular section.

NEEDLE THREAD TENSION

Before threading your machine, check to see how your thread is wound on the spool in comparison to how it will be fed through the thread path. If needed, switch the spool from horizontal to vertical or vice versa or try a thread stand so the thread will come off the spool properly.

When you thread your machine, place the thread into the take-up lever, then pass it between the tension discs. The thread *must pass between the discs* for them to do their job. If the presser foot is down while you're threading your machine, the thread will ride on the outside of the discs and there will be no tension on the thread at all, creating a mess and possibly jamming the machine.

The higher/tighter the tension setting, the more the tension discs will press together. Conversely, a lower setting will allow the discs to sit a smidge farther apart when the presser foot is down. If you are using a fine thread, the discs will need to be closer together (higher/tighter tension) to create sufficient tension.

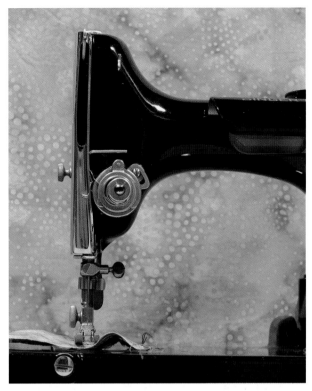

My Featherweight, born in 1934, is so old it doesn't have a numbered dial, just a knob! *"Right-y, tight-y; left-y loose-y."*

Tension Balance

- ✂ Black lines = fabric
- ✂ Gray thick line = batting
- ✂ Pink = needle thread
- ✂ Blue arrows = bobbin thread

- ✂ **left:** Bobbin thread shows on top: needle tension too tight OR bobbin tension too loose

- ✂ **center:** Balanced tension

- ✂ **right:** Needle tension shows on bottom: needle tension too loose OR bobbin thread too tight

If you are using a heavyweight machine quilting thread, however, you may need to loosen the tension to permit the heavier thread to pass through the discs without fraying or breaking.

The most notable exception (there's always at least one) is monofilament—the clear or smoke colored threads (they come in both polyester and nylon). These threads can stretch, so they tend to prefer a significantly *lower* tension than you would expect, considering how fine they are—perhaps as low as 2 or even 1 to feed smoothly.

Begin threading with the thread uptake lever in the "full-up" position. If you have a needle-up/needle-down button, use it, since it will return the lever to the full-up position. When the thread is ready to go into the uptake lever, press down gently on the thread on the top of the machine with one hand while using the other hand to pass the thread through the take-up lever and tension discs. Give a **gentle** tug to make sure the thread is properly seated between the discs. You'll hear or feel it "seat" itself properly. If you look closely, on some machines you can see a wire inside that looks a bit like part of a paperclip. If you tug gently on the tail of the thread, you'll see the wire move.

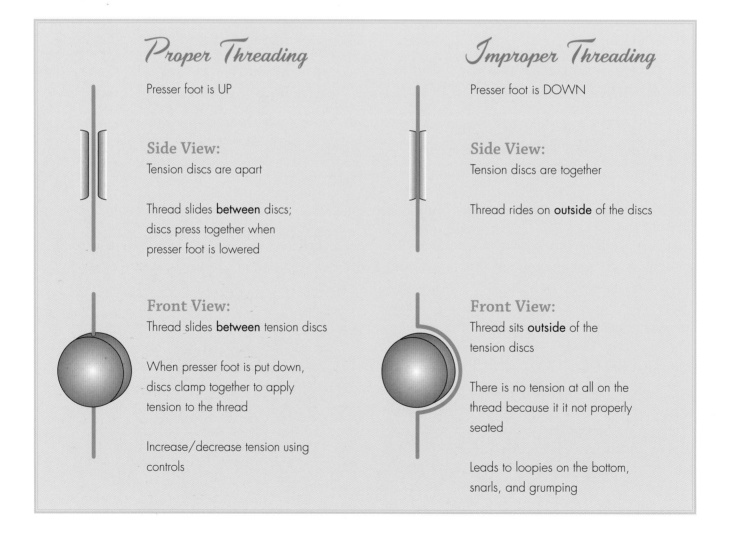

Proper Threading

Presser foot is UP

Side View:
Tension discs are apart

Thread slides **between** discs; discs press together when presser foot is lowered

Front View:
Thread slides **between** tension discs

When presser foot is put down, discs clamp together to apply tension to the thread

Increase/decrease tension using controls

Improper Threading

Presser foot is DOWN

Side View:
Tension discs are together

Thread rides on **outside** of the discs

Front View:
Thread sits **outside** of the tension discs

There is no tension at all on the thread because it it not properly seated

Leads to loopies on the bottom, snarls, and grumping

Most machine instructions will insist you thread your machine with the presser foot up the entire time. Sorry folks, but sometimes it is tricky getting big fingers into a tiny needle area. As long as I am certain I have properly seated the thread between the tension discs, I pull out enough thread to thread the needle, lower the presser foot while I get the thread through the eye of the needle, then lift the presser foot again to get ready to sew, double-checking that the thread is properly seated.

Alert! NEVER, EVER pull the needle thread when the presser foot is in the down position! This will do yucky stuff to the tension discs and settings (like mess them up). Especially with a free-motion foot on, it is sometimes easy to make this mistake because the presser foot does not touch the fabric when it is in the down position.

BOBBIN THREAD TENSION

Winding the bobbin with proper tension and seating the thread properly in the bobbin tension spring is just as important as having proper tension for the needle thread. Follow the instruction manual for your machine. In most cases, the thread should be wound snugly, with no loops, bubbles, or unevenness. If the thread on the bobbin is "squishy"—if you can easily depress it with your fingertip—it is probably not wound snugly or smoothly enough. It may be that the thread wasn't properly threaded for bobbin winding.

With the take-up lever in the full-up position, press the thread to the top of the machine as you pass it through the tension discs.

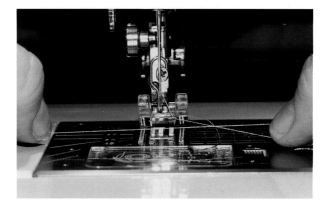

Holding on to the needle thread tail, take one stitch. Grab the needle thread with both hands as if you were going to floss your teeth. SWEEP the needle thread under the presser foot. It will catch the bobbin thread and sweep it right out to the back, where it is easy to reach.

Properly and improperly wound bobbins

There are two screws on this case: a black slot-head (|) that adjusts the tension on the spring and a silver Philips-head (+) that holds the spring in the case. You want to turn the screw that adjusts the tension.

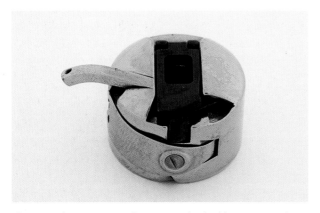

This case has an extra "finger" on the bobbin case with a small hole at the end.

Even though most tension issues can be solved by adjusting the needle thread tension, sometimes the bobbin case tension needs a tweak. If, after adjusting your needle tension, the bobbin thread continues to pop up to the top of the seam/stitching, you may need to tighten the bobbin tension. Turn the bobbin case tension screw to the right (clockwise). If your needle thread is pulled to the bottom no matter how loose you set the needle tension, you need to loosen the bobbin tension by turning the screw to the left (counterclockwise).

Remember: *"Right-y tight-y, left-y loose-y."*

Be sure to note the position of the screw before you start so you can set the tension back to where you began. Using the image of a clock as your guide, draw a picture of the tension screw slot. Turn the screw in five-minute increments and test the stitching each time until the tension is adjusted properly.

Some sewing machines have an extra "finger" on the bobbin case with a small hole at the end. By threading the bobbin through the hole, you can add tension to the bobbin thread without having to adjust the screw.

Tension Screw Slot

↳ Draw a circle; think of it as the face of a clock.

↳ Draw a line to show the starting position of your screw's slot.

↳ Here's the position of the screw on my machine after tightening by 10 minutes.

Troubleshooting

OK: despite your best efforts, something has gone amiss. Here's how to diagnose the problem.

A useful rule of thumb: If the loopies (that's another technical term) are on the top of the seam/stitching, the problem is probably in the bobbin thread path. If the loopies are underneath (where they usually are, lurking to be a nasty surprise when you think you're done and discover you aren't), the problem is in the thread path to the needle.

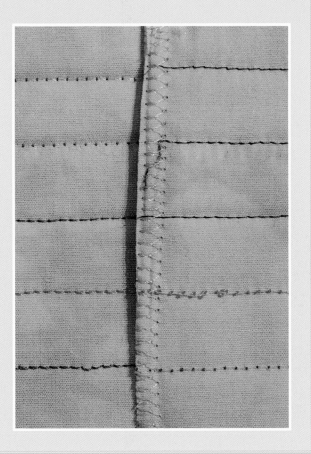

DIAGNOSING THE PROBLEM

Step A: Rethread both the top and bobbin threads, then run a tension-test seam sewing two patches together. If necessary, adjust the needle tension. If this doesn't work, move on to B and C.

Step B: Try different threads with the same fabric to see if the problem is a combination of that thread with that fabric.

Step C: Try the same threads on a different fabric to see if the same thread works fine with another fabric. Some fabrics have finishes on them that wreak havoc with tension.

Sometimes, a machine just "doesn't like" a certain type (or spool) of thread. Other times, it is the fabric that doesn't play nicely. Sometimes a spool of thread is old or brittle and just needs to be discarded.

WHAT TO DO

The best option is to remove the poor stitching and do it over. Sorry, I know, but it's true. The good news: it is quick and easy to unstitch poorly formed stitches.

Not as good, but it has been done (sorry, no true confessions here...I don't *dare* admit to this one! Ahem....) If tension is off and you don't discover it until after you've done a ton of quilting, use lightweight fusible interfacing or fused fabric on the back. This option is *not* a good one for a quilt that will receive a lot of use or be entered in a show, but it is *marginally* OK for a wallhanging that won't be subject to wear and tear and washing. You'll feel better if you just pick it out and do it right!

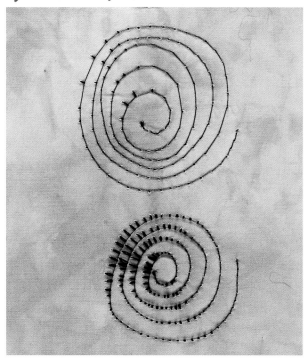

Bobbin side of spirals:

Top spiral: tension balanced but erractic and too-fast speed created long stitches and some eyelashes

Bottom spiral: loose needle tension; large loopies/eyelashes

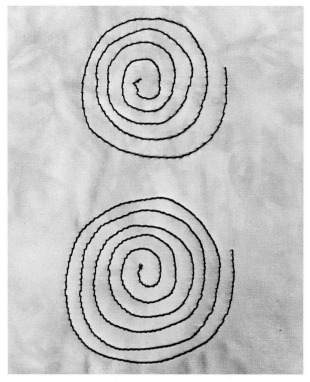

Needle side of spirals:

Top spiral: low needle-thread tension; bobbin

Bottom spiral: balanced tension

THE SPECIAL CASE OF EYELASHES AND CURVES

One of the most common problems to new free-motion stitchers is laddering or eyelashes. When going around curves, most new quilters tend to go faster (without realizing it). The change in speed leads to a change in the amount of pull on the needle thread, which adversely affects your formerly balanced tension. The result: lots of needle thread showing on the back, as in the top photo. It is similar to (accidentally) taking a curving off-ramp from the highway a bit too fast: you can feel the car pulling to the outside of the curve just as you can see extra thread pulled to the top.

The way to prevent eyelashes is to maintain a steady rhythm at all times, including when going around curves. As you become more practiced, you will find that you develop a personal rhythm that is comfortable for you. Listening to music with a steady beat can help you maintain a steady pace.

BROKEN NEEDLES AND BURRS

If you have broken a needle, you may have put a nick in the throat plate. Feel carefully for any rough spots. Sewing machine repair folks use crocus cloth, similar to an ultra-fine sandpaper, to smooth rough spots; track down some of this cloth at hardware stores or online and keep it on hand.

It is possible (unlikely, but possible) that there is a burr or snaggy spot (another technical term) in the thread path that is causing trouble. Make sure the thread hasn't jumped out of the uptake lever or tension discs in the needle thread path, or that the bobbin thread hasn't come unthreaded from the bobbin tension slot.

Your Workspace & Ergonomics

Make sewing easy on your body. If you are thinking, "Oh my back hurts," you won't be able to devote your full attention to your stitching. Make your tools, equipment, and surroundings work with you, not against you, so that you can do the best work possible and have fun!

Sewing Surface

I don't think it is possible to overemphasize the importance of a large, flat sewing surface. I know, I know—cabinets are expensive, bulky, and not everyone has room for them. Good news! There are alternatives.

OPTION A

The ideal setup is a work surface or cabinet where the sewing machine is recessed (dropped down) so that the surface of the machine bed is even with the top of the work surface. The entire weight of your work should be supported to the left (under your left elbow and to the left of the machine) and behind the machine.

OPTION B

You can modify an old table, flat door, or sheet of plywood by cutting an opening for your machine and creating a shelf under that surface.

You can order a made-to-fit acrylic insert or, as I did with my cabinet, use the extension table that comes with your machine on the surface of the table. A small ridge one half inch or less between your machine and the table surface shouldn't be a problem. If you are using plywood to make a table, you can use pre-made legs of 4x4 wood or pipe.

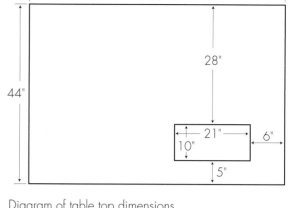

Diagram of table top dimensions

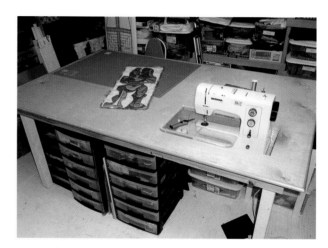

Deirdre Abbott made a table by sketching out her desired placement in the tabletop. She cut out the opening for her sewing machine and added rolling drawer units under the table.

OPTION C

Using straightforward plans, you can build your own setup. (See Design Alternatives under Resources, page 109, for Terry Hire's instructions.) If you use a slick varnish or paint or apply a melamine countertop, your table becomes a smooth, useful quilting surface.

OPTION D

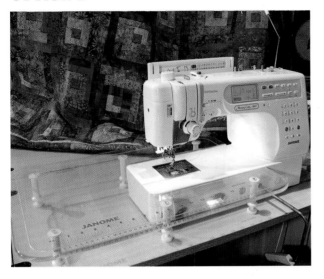

Any table can work *if* you have an extension table for your machine. Some machines come with an extension table or you can order one to custom fit your machine through your local quilt store or from catalogs. You want the table to extend about 12" to the left of the needle and about 4"–6" in front of and 6" or more behind the needle. You'll need this much space to be able to move your hands around during free-motion work without "falling off the edge."

A benefit to this setup is having a space under the table to stash your pins and scissors, plus you can use a clear extension table as a light box.

Option D works when a dedicated table isn't a viable option for your work space (like if it is in the dining room!). If you're handy with a saw, you can make a larger extension table, varnish it or apply laminate, and then store it under a bed or behind a door.

Just make sure that when you are working on a large piece, like a quilt, that the corners don't drape over the edges of the table. If you need to, use an ironing board, a bookcase, or even stacked boxes to create an extended, elevated work surface. If the fabric of your ironing board grabs at your quilt, tape a large plastic bag over the top.

Gravity works! If your quilt drops down just 3"–4" from the surface of the machine bed or over the edge of your table, the weight of the quilt is going to pull on the part of the quilt under the needle. In a worst-case scenario, this pulling can move the needle far enough out of place that it slams into the throat plate (not good at all).

Sitting Down

A good chair is important, too. To figure out the proper "home" position for your body, let your arms drop from your shoulders. When your forearms are at a right angle to your upper arms, they should rest on the sewing surface. Your chair seat should support your thighs at about a right angle to your back and your feet should touch a surface. A chair with an adjustable height and back such as a secretary's chair is ideal for fine-tuning your sitting position.

In this photo, you can see that my upper and lower arm form a right angle; my elbow is at (or a titch above) table height. My torso and thighs also make a right angle. Hidden inside the cabinet, my thighs and lower legs form a right angle. For this cabinet, I need the chair so high to be able to get my elbows level with the top that I need to perch my feet on a small platform.

You do NOT want to hunch over as in this picture.

Another no-no is chicken wings (elbows way up).

Once your arm and leg positions are set, place your hands on your hips and position your "driving foot" on the foot pedal. If you feel that hip raise up, it will cause your spine to curve instead of be straight, which will lead to a backache sooner or later. In this case, add a small book or box to prop up your other foot, which will level your hips and straighten out your spine.

Finally, center your body on the needle, not on the middle of the machine. If you sit with the needle to the left of the center of your body, you'll end up leaning to the left, and there comes that pesky backache again!

Think of this position as home base. Start and finish your sewing at home base, even though you're changing position while you sew or quilt.

Marginalia: Try moving your chair an inch or two back from your normal position to improve visibility behind the needle when free-motion stitching.

Understanding Good Foundations

Remember the analogy of painting the house? Foundations are part of the prep work: it's the sanding and spackling—not sexy, not fun, but necessary. In this section, I'll explain how to stabilize your work for appliqué and decorative stitching so that it looks good when you are done. There are four options: using stabilizers, using hoops, holding the work taut with your hands, or letting the quilt batting serve as the stabilizer.

Types of stabilizers

With the proliferation of home embroidery machines, the array of foundation choices has grown. You need to learn which to use for which sewing job. See the chart on pages 40–41. Most stabilizers are sold two ways—in sheets or on a roll (often used in digitized embroidery).

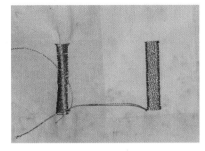

The sample on the left, stitched without stabilizer, is rippled, puckered, and basically looks yucky. After adding tear-away stabilizer and stitching with the exact same fabric, thread, and machine settings, the satin stitch on the right is flat, dense (no background showing through), and has nice edges.

Heat-away, tear-away, wash-away, and cut-away stabilizers

FOUNDATION CHOICES				
Product Type	**General Comments**	**Hand**	**Pros**	**Cons**
Tear-away	Woven and non-woven available; used underneath the area to be stitched; easily perforated by the machine needle; when stitched densely, especially on the edges of a design, easily removed by tearing away excess	Stabilizer underneath the stitched area remains, stiffening the remaining design area	Good when you can't wash the item or use high heat	Can pull and/or distort stitches if not removed carefully
Heat-away	Woven and non-woven available; removed by applying heat directly with an iron or heat gun; when done carefully, can be removed from underneath the stitching	When competely removed does not change the hand of the fabric or stitching	Does not require water to remove	Removal creates a lot of dust, which can end up stuck inside your stitching and be difficult to remove; in theory, could be used on top of a project with the pattern marked, but dust would still be a concern
Wash-away	Non-woven, both transparent and opaque; can be used on top in conjunction with a stabilizer beneath to keep stitches from sinking into fabric with pile such as velvet; can be used on the bottom in a hoop or when held taut; some water-soluble stabilizers wash out competely, while others "disintegrate" and leave fibers behind	If thoroughly rinsed, fabric remains supple; if not, can be stiff, but you could use this trait to sculpt and mold the fabric as desired	Does not require heat to remove	Some water-soluble stabilizers may require hot water or repeated rinsings to remove
Cut-away, Leave in	The type you see on the inside of baseball caps and commercially embroidered motifs on sweatshirts, fleece garments, and towels; both woven and non-woven	Leaves item stiff to rigid	Provides the strongest stabilizing for the most densely stitched designs; no distortion or mess because the excess is carefully trimmed —no pulling, no water, no heat	Too stiff for a bed/lap quilt, but OK in a wall quilt

OPPOSITE: NAIADS, detail, 18¼" x 49", made by the author

Product Type	General Comments	Hand	Pros	Cons
FOUNDATION CHOICES *(continued)*				
Freezer paper	Comes in 15" and 18" wide rolls; found at grocery stores usually near the foil and plastic wrap; iron with dry medium-heat to the wrong side of your project and stitch	When properly removed, no change to fabric hand at all	Inexpensive compared to other stabilizers; widely available	Not archival (acids in the paper); less easily removed than some other stabilizers; you'll get better fiddly points using proper stabilizer
Coffee filters & dryer sheets	Could be pin-, glue-, thread-, or spray basted		Difficult to remove competely	Not archival
Adding machine tape	Perfect for long, looooonnnggg strips of dense stitching			Not archival
Copy paper, tracing paper	Can be pin-, glue-, thread-, or spray-basted or just held beneath your fabric; tracing paper might wrinkle or bunch up but a spritz of basting spray can help it stay in place			Not archival

Marginalia: I used freezer paper in some of my Nourish the Body, Nourish the Soul quilt. I found that "real" stabilizer does a better job on those skinny points I seem to like so much and wish I'd used it on the whole quilt!

Because freezer paper is not archival, I wouldn't use it (and have bits of the paper and plastic coating left behind) on a piece I considered heirloom or top-dollar quality. For everyday quilts that are intended to be used and loved and that I don't expect to last for eternity, I'm OK with using freezer paper.

BASIC RULES OF THUMB

There are some general guidelines to keep in mind when using stabilizers.

 ❧ DO A TEST using scraps of your fabric, thread, and a bit of stabilizer before working on the "real thing."

 ❧ Make sure your stabilizer is suitable to the task. Don't use wash-away stabilizer if you don't want your project to be soaked. Don't use heat-away stabilizer with heat-sensitive products such as synthetic sheer fabrics and polyester threads that may melt.

 ❧ For heavier fabrics, usually you'll need a less-heavy stabilizer.

 ❧ If your stitching is very dense, you'll need heavier stabilizer to prevent distortion. You can use two layers of regular stabilizer instead of one heavy-duty layer. You may want to spray baste or glue-stick the two layers together.

 ❧ Before removing wash-away or heat-away stabilizer, trim away as much of the stabilizer as possible to eliminate unnecessary residue.

Hoops

It is possible to stabilize cloth in a hoop instead of, or in addition to, using a stabilizing product. By holding the fabric taut, the hoop prevents (or at least reduces) the puckering, shrinkage, and warping that would otherwise occur with dense stitching.

There are three basic kinds of hoops suitable for use on a sewing machine. In all cases, you want a hoop that is less in diameter than double the distance from the sewing machine needle to the housing on the right-hand side of your machine. If the hoop is larger, you won't be able to reach the center of the hoop with your sewing machine needle.

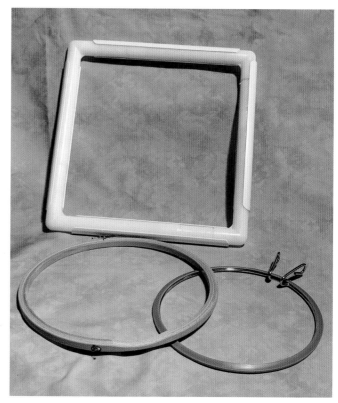

Clockwise from top: Q-snap, spring clamp, and wooden machine embroidery hoops

SPRING CLAMP

These hoops consist of a plastic ring with a springy circular metal ring with two "wings" or handles that you press together to set it into the groove in the plastic ring (purple hoop, on page 42). These come in assorted sizes. They have a flat profile, so they slide easily underneath the raised presser foot, and the handles can be used to steer the hoop as you free-motion stitch. However, if you press too hard on both handles, the spring can pop out of the outer ring.

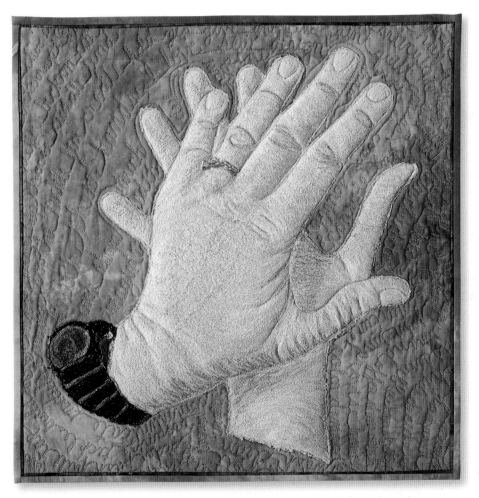

WITH THESE HANDS, 14" x 14", made by the author. I traced the outline of my hands (enlarged on the computer screen, which I used as a light box) onto heat-away stabilizer. I hooped the stabilizer with two layers of tulle (a fine synthetic mesh) in a spring clamp. I used 14 colors of pinks and browns, plus a pool blue and gray thread, to create the appliqué. There is no other fabric in the hands—just the tulle and lots of thread. Because the thread-appliqué hands are larger than the hoop, I needed to reposition the embroidery sandwich as I moved around the hands.

In Bijagos Warrior, a quilt based on a photo I took in Guinea-Bissau in 1982 (on the west coast of Africa, just south of Senegal), I quilted the central figure to a blended batting. I then cut out the figure (gasp! gulp!).

WOODEN MACHINE EMBROIDERY

These wooden hoops feature a screw tension and are similar to hand embroidery hoops. These hoops have a small scooped out area to make it easier to slide them under the presser foot. The screw mechanism makes it easy to get a smooth, taut surface no matter how thick your fabric is.

Q-SNAP

Q-Snap hoops are made of white plastic pipe that creates a square or rectangular shape and are usually used for hand quilting. They have C-shaped pieces that snap onto the pipe sides to secure the fabric. Too thick to fit under the presser foot, you need to hoop the fourth side of your fabric while at the machine. Hooping the fabric this way is awkward, but if you want to make long lines of decorative stitching or free-motion embroidery without overlapping segments, you won't have to re-hoop as often.

Holding It Taut

Another stabilizing option is to hold the fabric taut yourself. This requires a fair bit of coordination and will result in more (and uncontrolled) shrinkage than other methods. However, there may be instances where it is a useful technique. I held heavy water-soluble stabilizer by hand to make the hair on the figures in BEDTIME because I wanted strands of hair longer than could be accommodated by any hoop under a sewing machine.

Batting as Stabilizer

Batting can also serve as a stabilizer. The good news is that you can do your threadwork and quilt it at the same time. The bad news is that you will have a LOT of thread tails to bury. An additional caution is that you must be especially careful to avoid distorting the quilt surface.

I spliced the background together, and added more layers of batting underneath the central figure to create a three-dimensional surface. The man facing us is stitched to the main batt around the edges of his body, arms, chin, and shorts. The remainder of the quilt is heavily quilted.

BEDTIME, detail of thread-painted hair

Marking Tools

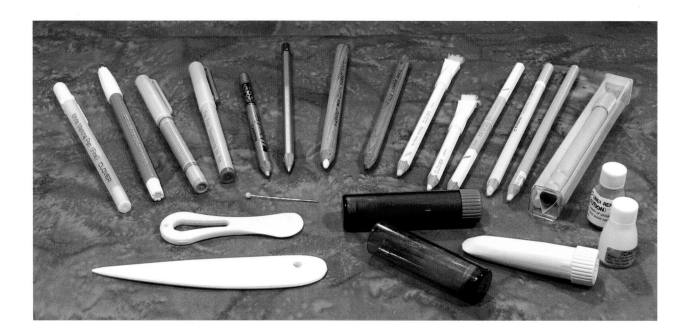

Let's be honest here: marking a quilt for free-motion embroidery and quilting is right up there in the fun category with getting a tooth filled. But marking is a necessary task depending on the style and design of the stitching or quilting. The key to making this job less of a chore is selecting the right tool for the job. Some marking tools are suited only for designs that will be stitched immediately, while others are better suited to a project that will take a long time to finish or that requires absolute precision (think ornate and symmetrical designs).

There are five types of marking tools:
- ✄ pencils
- ✄ chalk
- ✄ pens
- ✄ scoring tools
- ✄ transfer paper

You also have the option of using a "no-mark" design.

Marking Alerts

Alert 1! For ALL tools, TEST, TEST, TEST on your project fabrics, no matter what tool you choose! Different tools will react to different fabrics differently. What worked perfectly on one project might not work at all on the next!

Marginalia: How do you test? Use a SCRAP of each fabric that will be marked (not the project itself!) and mark it with your choice of tool(s), noting which is which. Then subject the scrap to "fabric torture"—iron it, steam it, ignore it. Do everything you aren't supposed to do, then see if the markings wash out. If they do, you're fine. If one of those processes causes a problem, be extra sure not to use that process on your project while it is marked.

Alert 2! There is something in **yellow** pigment (in both chalk and pencils) that makes it particularly difficult to remove from fabric. If yellow is the only marking color that will show up on your fabrics, be extra sure to test for removability. Sometimes blue can be "iffy" but it is less troublesome than yellow.

Marking Tools

PENCILS can be pencils made specifically for quilters, designed to be used on and (in theory) easily removed from fabric; lead pencils (regular or mechanical); or artists' colored pencils.

CHALK has been used for centuries in garment making and it works well for quilters, too. Tailor's chalk is designed for use on the wrong side of fabric and may leave traces behind, so a better option for quilters is a chalk tool that combines a tracing wheel with chalk or an old-fashioned "pouncing" tool, a pad filled with a powdery substance to tamp over a stencil.

PENS are either felt-tip or roller-ball style with a special "ink" that washes out or "evaporates" into the air. The most common are the blue water-erasable and purple air-erasable pens. More recently on the market are white pens designed for marking on dark fabrics that can be removed with either heat or water.

SCORING TOOLS such as the Clover® Hera™ marker make incised lines or creases on the fabric. This works best on a quilt after it is basted. The line lasts only long enough to go from marking to the sewing machine. However, if you want a quick, simple guideline and your fabric is not so visually busy that you can't see the score mark, it's a great method because you don't have to remove it! I have used my fingernail, the back side of a seam ripper tip, my trusty bamboo skewer, a bone folder, and even a blunt needle or pin to make these marks.

TRANSFER PAPER is similar to dressmaker's marking paper and is used like carbon paper. The most widely available brands are Transdoodle and Saral and they come in white, blue, yellow, red, and graphite. I prefer white and blue. As always, use caution with anything yellow. You can buy 5-packs of 8½" x 11" sheets (one of each color), single-color packages (harder to find), or rolls. The Transdoodle brand comes in large rolled sheets. Transfer paper is available at art supply stores and online. This is how to use it:

- Place the quilt top on a firm surface (a table, not a padded ironing surface).

- Place the quilt design on to the quilt top, aligning it carefully. Pin the top edges of the quilt design paper in place.

- Lift up the quilt design paper and slide a piece of transfer paper underneath, chalk side down.

Note: Some folks like to use a light box or tape everything to a window (a de facto light box) to make it easier to align the pattern with the top. I don't have a large enough light box or sliding glass door, so I use the lift and place method.

    Trace over the design lines using a stylus, pencil, ballpoint pen (one that has run out of ink is ideal), or tip of a knitting needle to transfer the design to the quilt top.

How to Mark a Quilt

Chalk-like lines are ideal for the way I work. I often don't figure out how I want to quilt something until the quilt is partly quilted. The chalk comes off fairly easily, so this wouldn't be a good choice for marking something like an Amish quilting design that will take a long time to quilt, as the chalk will rub off before the quilting is complete. But for my purposes, it works well.

Removing Markings

Remove as much of the markings as you can with brushing (for pencil and chalk). A stiff paintbrush (dedicated for quilt mark removal), a soft toothbrush, or a terry washcloth all work well.

For anything lap-sized or smaller, hold the finished quilt face *down* under cool running water. This permits the pencil/chalk/water-soluble pen to wash into the sink or tub instead of soaking into the batting. Squeeze out as much water as possible and transfer the quilt to your washing machine or sink.

For LARGE quilts (anything larger than you can manage to rinse out yourself), place the finished quilt in the washing machine, use a gentle cycle, and set the water temperature to cool. Run the quilt through a prewash or wash cycle without any soap.

Then wash the quilt using a quilt-friendly soap or detergent and warm water on the gentle cycle. Use the "extra rinse cycle" if you have it; if not, run the quilt through the wash cycle a second time without soap.

BE SURE THE MARKS ARE GONE **BEFORE** you dry the quilt on low in the dryer or hang or block it to dry because heat can permanently set some marks.

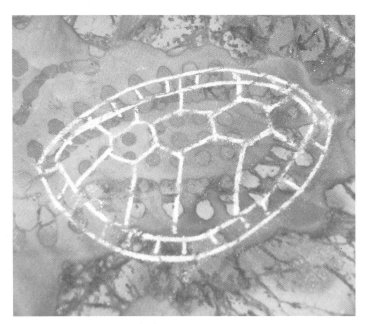

Design traced in chalk

PINK WREATH, 18" x 18", and detail. Made by the author. I used silver Superior Glitter™ thread to quilt the feathered wreath and a dark pink 60-wt. Mettler silk-finish cotton for the stippling. You can see the stippling, but it doesn't distract the viewer from the focal point—the silver wreath, fans, and lines.

If you want a precise quilting design such as in this feathered wreath project, you'll want to mark your top before it is batted and basted. You get a much more crisp, precise line when marking the top on a hard surface.

Appliqué

Skill is how you close the gap between what you can see in your mind's eye and what you can produce; the more skill you have, the more sophisticated and accomplished your ideas can be.

--Twyla Tharp, *The Creative Habit*, page 63

In appliqué (from French, "to apply") we are applying one piece of fabric on top of another. Reverse appliqué also applies one fabric to another, but the motif or design element is cut out of the background. In effect, the background is appliquéd (applied) on top of the motif.

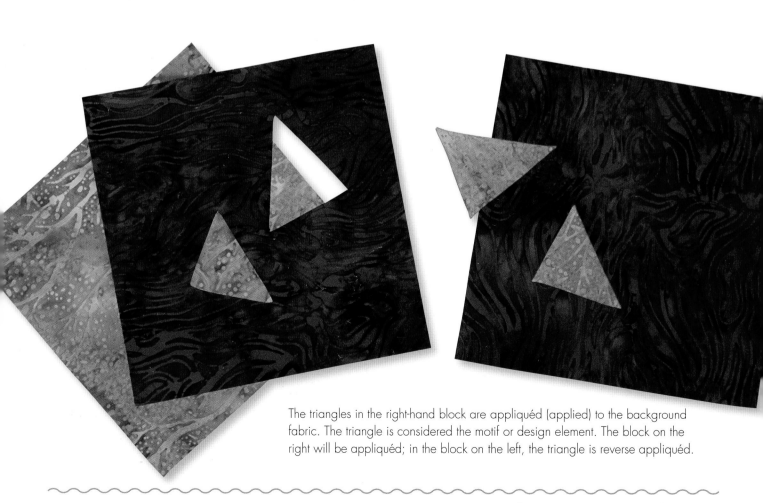

The triangles in the right-hand block are appliquéd (applied) to the background fabric. The triangle is considered the motif or design element. The block on the right will be appliquéd; in the block on the left, the triangle is reverse appliquéd.

The Look of the Appliqué: What Works for Your Project

When selecting an appliqué technique, consider both the look you want and the end use of the project. Different techniques result in a different look and feel of the finished item. The thread choices will depend on which technique you use.

Some methods leave fuzzy, soft edges while others are crisp and clean, even bold. Some appliqué methods are more sturdy (able to survive fort-making and the laundry); others are more suitable for wall quilts.

One of the most important considerations is the stiffness factor. Quilts to snuggle under need to be soft and, well, snuggly! Wall quilts, however, may benefit from appliqué that adds a certain amount of stiffness and flatness, provided you want a flat quilt. On the other hand, you might *want* a quilt, or at least part of a quilt, to be deliberately wavy and lumpy to add textural dimension.

For garments that are supple and drape nicely over the body, you'll want to use an appliqué technique that doesn't add significant stiffness.

To Turn or Not to Turn

In turned-edge appliqué the edge of the motif fabric is turned under and the subsequent fold is stitched to the background using one of several techniques. Motifs are cut with a seam allowance. In raw-edge appliqué the cut edge of the motif is cut without a seam allowance and left unturned.

You'll want to consider which fabric will serve as the background and which fabric(s) as the appliqué. Whenever possible, I like to have the lighter fabric underneath with darker fabrics on top. This way, I don't have shadow-through (the darker fabric showing through on the front) changing the appearance of the top. In some cases, this means I'll want to use reverse appliqué.

However, reverse appliqué can make a motif seem recessed, and that may not be the look I want. I can compensate by using a light appliqué on a dark background and either trimming away the background layer underneath (the traditional technique used in hand appliqué), adding an underlining, or facing the appliqué to prevent shadow-through.

To Trim or Not to Trim?

In traditional hand appliqué, the background fabric was trimmed away to make hand quilting easier and to prevent shadow-through from dark fabrics.

With machine work, we have a choice: trim or leave it alone. Both ways work, both have their advocates. The reasons to trim are the same as for hand appliqué: to make quilting easier, to permit the appliqué to "loft" or rise up above the background, and to prevent shadowing from seam allowances.

Some quilters feel that leaving the background in place makes the piece more stable and, therefore, easier to sew, whether it is a block, a large panel, or an entire quilt top.

How to choose? Do a test! Every quilt is a learning experience. If you're not wild about the results, try another way next time.

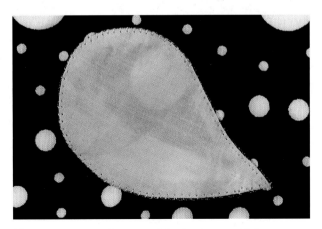

Here you can see the print of the background fabric through the pink appliqué.

Understanding and Using Color in Thread

Thread is SO much more than just what sews the appliqué in place! It creates line, shape, and dimension. It becomes a design element.

STITCH DENSITY/APPEARANCE

First, let's look at **stitch density**: how close (or far apart) the stitches are on a quilt (whether at the embroidery or quilting stage). In this thread sampler, I used threads ranging from 100-wt. (very fine) silk to 30-wt. heavy cotton, all in medium browns (or as close as I could get from my stash of thread).

Across the top of the sampler, I wrote the name of the thread and the weight (if listed; if not, I guessed). First, I stitched a single line diagonally, followed by a simple free-motion vertical zigzag. Next, I tested a stipple stitch (keeping the spacing in the curlicues the same no matter what size thread), a leaf sprig, pebbles, and then left a dangly bit of thread so I could see what the thread looks like hanging off the spool.

The sampler shows that fine threads are well-suited to small, densely stitched designs without drawing undue attention to themselves. For example, if you want to stitch the background densely so that a decorative motif will "pop," you can use a very fine thread without having it visually distract the viewer from the focal point: the motif.

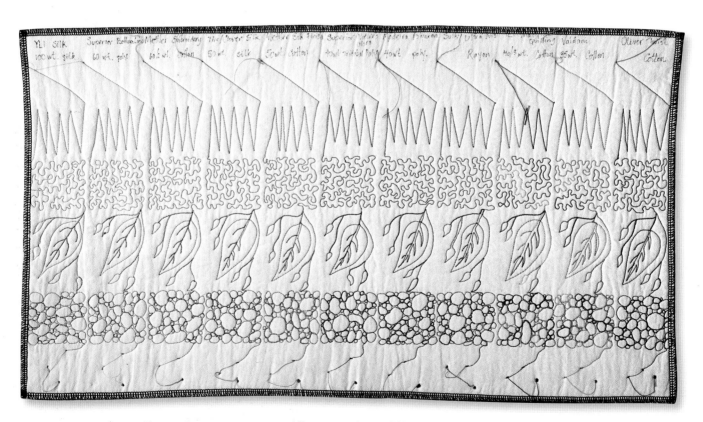

THREAD SAMPLER, comparing different weights and fibers. On the far left, the fine 100-wt silk looks wimpy in most of the designs, and doesn't have much presence except for the densely stitched pebbles. Moving to the far right, to the heaviest cotton thread, the stippling and pebbles look too heavy, almost globbed onto the surface, but the zigzag and the simple line of stitching have presence.

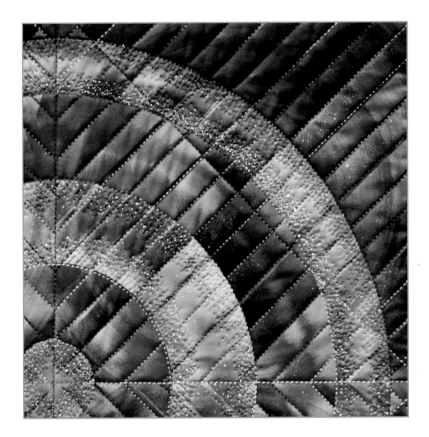

CIRCLE POINT, 10" x 10", and detail, made by Gloria Hansen, Hightstown, New Jersey. Gloria makes her artwork on the computer, using software to create the colors, lines, and shapes. She uses thread to accentuate the transitions and lines in her computer-created imagery.

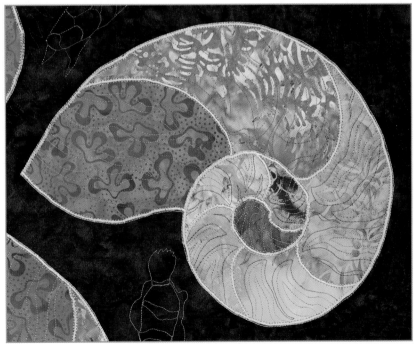

UNDER THE BALI SEA, 42" x 42", and detail, made by author

CURL I, 20" x 24", © 1999 Jane Sassaman.
Jane is a master at using thread color to influence the viewer's eye. Working primarily with solid fabrics, she uses black, white, and shades of green thread to create a light source on the right side of her quilt. The triple rows of white on the jaggedy edges exaggerate the contrast between the mauve and black and create the sharp, bold edges for which Jane is famous.
Photo by Gregory Gantner.

THE TIDE IS HIRE, 51" x 51", made by the author (in the International
Quilt Festival Collection)

NOURISH THE BODY, NOURISH THE SOUL, 64" x 64", made by the author

On the other hand, if you want the thread to be part of the focal point, you can use a thick or bright thread. In PINK WREATH'S case the silver holographic thread definitely says, "Look at me!" (See photos page 49.)

Thread can also be a design element on its own. Look at "before" and after pictures of the Pineapple block in NOURISH THE BODY, NOURISH THE SOUL.

After

Before

The blocks could stand alone as is, but the bold magenta line of satin stitching brings added attention to the line of the patterns.

Before

After

USING THREAD COLOR TO TONE DOWN, SHADE, AND HIGHLIGHT

The color of the thread can be used to modify the appearance of the underlying fabric—to tone down something that is too bright, to add red tones (once the quilt is put together) to a fabric that appears too blue, to add depth, and to highlight.

In AUTUMN BOREALIS, I selected a light source (upper right), pretending the sun was off to the right. The side of the quilted leaves facing in that direction would be brighter, while the under or back side of those leaves would be darker.

RIGHT: In BEDTIME (detail), I created depth and dimension on the bedpost with thread. Instead of piecing different browns to create the dark and light sides, I used a brown thread darker than the fabric on the shaded side of the post, and a lighter yellow-brown on the side near the lamp.

BELOW: AUTUMN BOREALIS, detail. I used five different shades of green ranging from light to dark to quilt the leaf shapes, then used a single line of neon green thread to accent the upper edge of the leaf where it catches the light. Instead of looking garish (as the neon threads can when they are massed on a spool), the neon thread catches the light in the room and pops that edge just like a glint of sunlight.

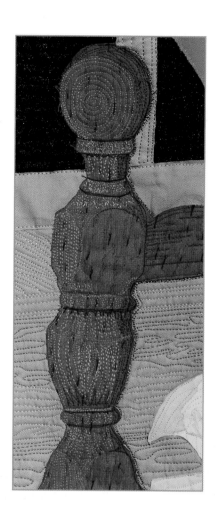

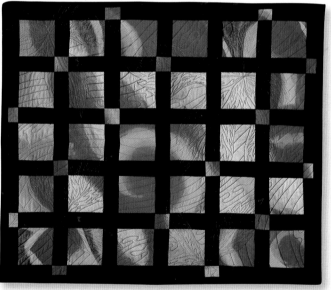

AUTUMN BOREALIS, 22" x 26", made by the author

COLOR BANDS SAMPLER

The color bands sampler illustrates the ways colored thread can affect one's perception of the underlying color. I picked fabric in six basic colors plus gray, white, and black, then selected threads that matched those colors as closely as possible. On the top/needle side of the quilt, I used a 40-wt trilobal polyester (a shiny polyester with a high sheen similar to rayon) and I used a matte 60-wt cotton in the bobbin.

As you look at the sampler from left to right, the threads are gray (in the gray border), black, red, orange, yellow, green, blue, purple, and white. I left a strip about a half-inch wide unstitched in each segment to show the plain fabric.

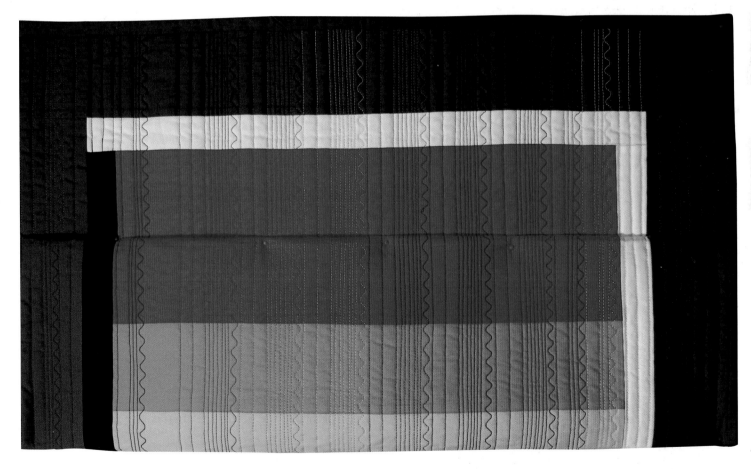

Where the thread is stitched about ½" apart, there is a slight change in the appearance of the underlying fabric color, but where the straight lines are a scant ⅛" apart, there is a distinct change in one's perception of the fabric.

The quilt is rolled so you can compare the effect of the thinner bobbin thread (top half of photo) with the thicker needle thread (bottom half of photo). The heavier, shinier thread, makes a greater change in the appearance of the fabric color underneath.

Butted stitching

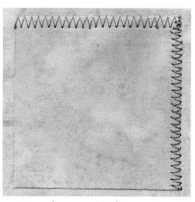

Overlap/log-cabin stitching

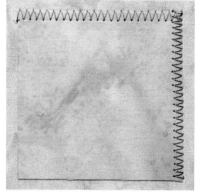

Mitered zigzag stitching

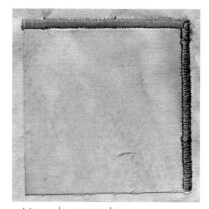

Mitered satin stitching

Stitching Options

Once you have selected a technique and a thread, it's time to sew down the appliqué.

To get ready for stitching, affix prepared appliqué pieces to your background, layering the pieces from back to front. You can use pins, glue stick, basting spray, or fusing to hold the pieces in place for stitching.

Whether your design is a simple flower or a complex landscape, always start with the background and more distant pieces (sky, distant mountains, foothills), followed by the middle zone (house in the distance, but in front of the foothills), with the foreground last (flowers, animals in the pasture). If your appliqué pattern has pieces that overlap, the pieces on the top go on last.

STRAIGHT STITCH

Straight stitch is the easiest and probably the fastest way to sew down an appliqué. Just stitch! If you will be doing extensive threadwork at either the embellishment or quilting stages, the straight stitch is a good option because the stitching will blend in with the embroidery or quilting. However, if you are going for a mock-hand appliqué look, this isn't the option for you.

BLIND HEM, MINI-BLANKET, OR ZIGZAG STITCH

These stitches can be used for mock hand appliqué, also called invisible appliqué. To achieve the least obtrusive look, select a thread that disappears into the appliqué. If you are nearsighted like I am, you can lay several threads on top of the appliqué fabric and remove your glasses; the thread you can see the least (or not at all!) is the best one. If you have good eyesight, squint or borrow someone's glasses to deliberately blur your vision.

Stitch in the ditch next to the appliqué (just a whisker from the edge of the appliqué piece, on the background), and the needle will swing onto the appliqué. Adjust your machine to the narrowest "zig" available that still takes a strong stitch into the appliqué.

SATIN STITCH

Satin stitch is a densely packed zigzag stitch. Depending on the density of your satin stitch, you may very well want to use a stabilizer because satin stitching can distort and buckle the background fabric. The wider the satin stitch and the more on the bias of the fabric it is, the more likely the stitching is to distort the fabric.

Satin stitch can be done with the feed dogs up or free motion with the feed dogs down. It is easier to get a consistent stitch length with feed dogs up, but with (a lot of) practice, you can do it free motion. You can vary the width of the satin stitch as you are stitching, but the smoothness of the transition will depend on your machine's preset increments of change.

Satin stitching corners

To turn a corner, stitch up to the end of the side. With the needle in the down position at the outside corner, lift the presser foot and pivot the fabric. Lower the presser foot and set the stitch width to about .8 or 1.0. Increase width quickly as you stitch, creating a mitered corner of satin stitching. By having stitched to the outside edge of the piece on the first side, you won't have any show-through of background fabric.

Mitered satin stitching can be quite tricky to do well as you can see from the photo (page 60). When you use all the same color of thread (which would be the usual case) you have a little more fudging room.

I use this method for the tips of leaves as well as 90-degree corners. I taper the stitch width on both sides of the tips (page 60). This takes practice. Just do it and you'll get better.

If your sewing machine has a mitered corner triangle programmed into it, stitch the corner using that decorative stitch, then switch back to the satin stitch.

Satin stitching curves

You need to stop with the needle down and pivot your fabric in tiny increments to satin stitch curves smoothly.

Leave the needle down on the "hip" or convex side of the curve. Overlap at the "waist" or concave side of the curve. See UNDER THE BALI SEA photos on page 53.

If the edges of your satin stitching aren't quite as smooth as you'd like, or if you just want a sharper, ultra-crisp, bold edge, you can outline stitch on either or both sides of the satin stitching. I first saw this technique used by Jane Sassaman and use the technique myself. It takes a LONG TIME to finish, but makes a huge difference in the final look.

Hint: You can use the hand appliquér's trick to give the illusion of an even sharper point by adding a TINY vertical stitch at the tip of the leaf, or angling the outlining just a teensy, tiny bit out from the point of the leaf.

THE TIDE IS HIRE, detail. Each of the appliquéd waves is satin stitched. I outlined the top of the satin stitching with thread a shade lighter than the satin stitching, then underlined that same row with thread a shade darker. It took about eight hours to do just the outlining with the feed dogs up, but it was worth it! Full quilt shown on page 55.

Decorative-Stitch Appliqué

True Confessions time again, folks: how many of you have machines with decorative stitches, yet you almost never use them? Many if not most of you, I'll bet! By using the most basic utility stitches such as the blind hem or overcast stitch, stretch stitch, and zigzag, you can achieve a range of decoration. Once you've seen the possibilities, a whole new option for appliqué opens up!

As with any appliqué or quilting, the more thread you use on the surface, the stiffer the final product will be. Openwork decorative stitches will be more flexible, and therefore more suitable and/or comfortable in garments and cuddly quilts. On wallhangings, stiffness may be a virtue, not a vice.

Marginalia: Like satin stitching, many decorative stitches will cause your appliqué to distort if you don't use a stabilizer.

Think about how obvious you want the decorative stitching to be. Each of us has different preferences regarding contrast and subtlety. In my LEAF SAMPLER, I've stitched the same leaf six ways. It's like bringing home a small can of paint to try on the living room wall. You need to try different options and actually **see** them to find out what you like with the set of fabrics you have on hand. Remember? *Make visual decisions visually.*

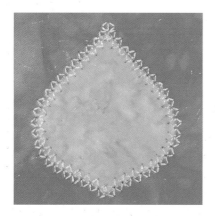

1. Semi-solid background and semi-solid leaf, thread blending with the leaf

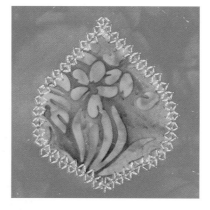

2. Semi-solid background, print fabric leaf, thread blending with the leaf

3. Semi-solid background, print fabric leaf, thread contrasting with both the leaf and the background

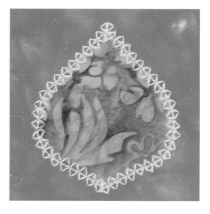

4. Busy background, semi-solid leaf, thread blending with the leaf

5. Busy background, semi-solid leaf, thread contrasting with leaf

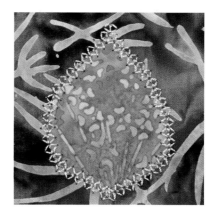

6. Busy background, busy leaf, thread contrasting with both

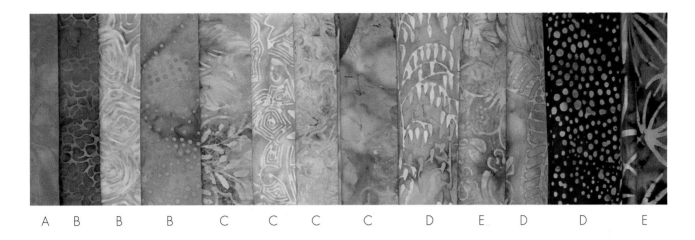

A   B   B   B   C   C   C   C   D   E   D   D   E

Visual Texture

A solid fabric is the least "busy" of all fabrics: by definition, it is plain. A monochromatic, or one-color, print such as this batik "solid" (A) or print (B) adds a bit more visual activity, but not a lot. Larger scale prints with smooth edges (C) are busier than A or B, but not as busy as a similarly colored print with sharp edges (D) or a multicolored print with large variations in light and dark, hue (color), and size/shapes (E).

Contrast and Value

Traditional quilts are all about strong contrasts. Think of the crispness of a blue and white quilt; the sharp contrast accentuates the intricate piecing. The same is true of scrappy Log Cabin blocks where one side is light, the other dark. On the other hand, colorwash quilts are all about blending, where the lines of piecing are blurred to create smooth transitions from one fabric to the next.

What is going on in contrast is actually a change in value, that is, how light or dark the fabrics are. There is a saying that is, oh, so true:

Value does all the work, but color gets all the credit.

Do a Stitch-Out to See What Works

Below is an example of a stitch-out for a quilt using a blue solid batik on a darker blue dotted batik. I tested four threads in blues, four in plums and pinks. Because the fabric was dark, I cut file folder labels into small segments and wrote down on each which thread brand, color, and stitch settings (width and length) were used. If I needed to change the tension, I noted that, too. It is easy to see which threads disappear (the Mettler 50-wt cotton); which make a subtle line (the navy and dark purple); which are really bold (that pink!); and how the variegated thread's stripes stitch out at different widths.

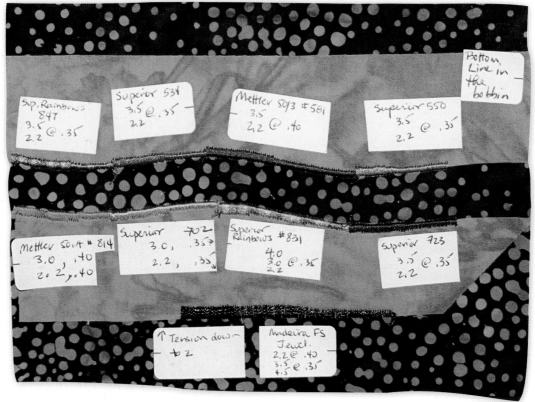

Machine Quilting

Both the traditional and the modern are available to you. . . . let me reiterate that it's all on the table, all up for grabs. Isn't that an intoxicating thought? I think it is. Try any... thing you like, no matter how boringly normal or outrageous. If it works, fine. If it doesn't, toss it. Toss it even if you love it.

Stephen King, *On Writing* (p. 196-197)

The skills of free-motion stitching are much the same whether done at the embellishment/embroidery stage or at the quilting stage. The major difference is how the top is stabilized. If you wait until you have added batting and backing, those materials stabilize the quilt top and prevent unwanted distortion (for the most part). The same rules apply: the softer your fabric, the stronger the stabilizer you will need; and the more densely stitched the piece is, the stronger the stabilizer you will need.

Whether you are embroidering, quilting, making motifs, or working on a pictorial quilt, an appliqué with pictorial elements, an abstract piece, or a geometric quilt, there are common elements you will want to consider when picking your quilting design and thread. The two major factors are the technical requirements and aesthetic considerations—which design suits your quilt top and matches your quilting skills.

RIGHT: FIELDS OF GOLD, detail, 20" x 22¼", made by the author

The Quilt Top

Here's how to have a flat quilt top, a smooth backing, how to baste the quilt well, work comfortably, use tools and "aids" that will help you, and employ a few tips and tricks to make your life easier when quilting.

It is much easier to end up with a flat quilt if you begin with a flat quilt top. Sometimes after piecing or appliquéing your quilt, you end up with ripples and even "A-cups." If you don't want that bulge there when the quilt is done, your life will be much easier if you correct the problem *before* basting the quilt.

The Backing

You'll also want the backing to be flat and wrinkle-free to minimize the possibility of quilting tucks into it. Backing fabric with a busy print will hide your stitching, so it may be your choice if you are new to free-motion quilting and are concerned about the evenness of your stitches. A solid or near-solid fabric will show the stitching much more. That's why a whitework quilt was considered the pinnacle of a young woman's quilting career in the nineteenth century—EVERY stitch showed!

The Batting

What's the best batting to use for your project? The answer is the dreaded "it depends"—on the look you want for your quilt. Do you want it to look puckery and old-timey, like a 1930s-era comfy quilt? Do you want it flat and smooth? Do you want loft and definition to show off the quilting and perhaps the shine of silk and satin fabrics in the top? Do you like to do a lot of quilting (I do!) or not so much? In each case, you would want to select a different batting.

Look at the batting package. It will tell you how close or far apart you can quilt without running into trouble.

COTTON: Different cotton batts will give a different look. Some shrink, which leads to the puckery look of antique and 1930s-era quilts. Some companies offer bleached and unbleached versions, with the former being more suitable to quilts with a lot of white or light colored fabrics. Some companies are now making black cotton or cotton-blend batts, which are useful for quilts made of mostly deep, dark colors.

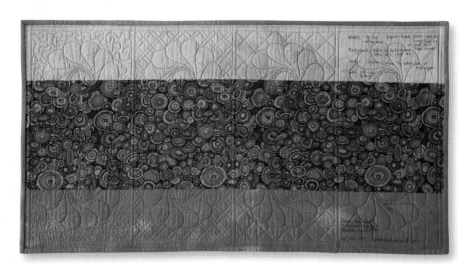

The different backings used on my WREATH SAMPLER illustrate how much (or little) quilting can show. I used a peachy-pink thread in the bobbin that matches the hand-dyed fabric on the bottom. You can see the quilting, but the thread doesn't stand out like it does on the blue fabric. On the busy print, nothing shows!

POLY: The new generation of polyester batts are needlepunched and look, feel, and behave more like cotton. They come in bright white and also in a very dark black. They don't shrink at all and usually have a very flat appearance when quilted. The puffy poly batts are a nightmare to machine quilt well; I avoid them!

WOOL: Wool is a dream to hand quilt (like a hot knife through butter!) and easy to machine quilt. These batts require basting a bit more closely than cotton, but like cotton, wool and wool-blend batts snuggle up to cotton tops and backings. They are warm, lightweight, and resilient. Pure wool batts are more likely to beard (where unsightly wisps of batting wick up through the weave of the top), so they may not be suitable for dark quilts (unless you can find a charcoal wool batt). Because wool has a "memory," it doesn't hold a crease the way cotton batts do. Many quilters who enter shows like a wool batt for that very reason. Wool batts are available in 100 percent, 80–20, and 60–40 blends. Wool batts usually cost more than cotton or polyester batts of comparable size.

OTHER: There are now many variations on the theme of battings—silk (very expensive but very soft and supple), cotton-silk blends, cotton-wool blends, bamboo, and man-made fibers. Major quilt magazines periodically review what is currently on the market.

Basting

The goal in basting a quilt sandwich, composed of the backing, batting or other "in the middle" layer, and the top, is to keep all three layers together without shifting, puckering, pleating, or other quilty misbehavior.

Traditionally, quilts were hand basted with thread. However, I can guarantee you two things if you thread-baste by hand: the thread will snag on the presser foot; and, no matter how you try to avoid it, you will stitch through the basting thread, making it nearly impossible to remove. The good news is that we now have a wide variety of alternatives to hand basting.

No matter how you baste, you want to have the same tension on all three layers. If you pull the backing taut but the batting layer and top are smoothed on, when you release the backing it will contract, creating ripples on the top and making your life more difficult. The opposite is also true: if the back and batting are smooth, but you over-stretch the top of the quilt, you'll introduce batting lumps and pleats on the back.

Many references suggest basting at least every four inches. If you are working with all cotton (backing, batting, and thread), this is a good distance. My rule of thumb is that if I put my palm (or fist) down on the quilt and it is touching a pin, I have basted closely enough. If your *batting* is more slippery (wool or some polyesters) or your *fabric* is more slippery (such as shiny silks, some polyesters, and cotton sateens), you may want to use more pins or use one of the other basting alternatives that provides a more secure bond between the layers. You can easily use 400 or more pins on a lap quilt! I keep mine opened in a dish for ease of use.

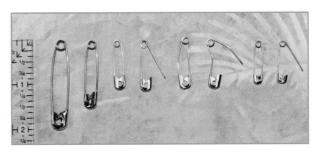

Safety pins work extremely well for basting a quilt. Use the Size 1 (1" long or about the size of a US quarter). They're large enough to go through all three layers, but not so large that they leave large holes in the fabric. The "Baby Bear" pins in the middle, are "just right." I prefer the bent ones as they distort the quilt surface less than the straight ones.

Depending on size, you can baste your quilt by smoothing it out on the floor, on a table, or a design wall. I prefer to use my work table, as it is easier on my back and knees.

If you are working on a floor, use painter's tape to hold the smoothed-out backing to the floor. (It leaves less residue than regular masking tape.) Smooth on the batting and finally the top. Pin from the center working out. Leave the pins OPEN until the entire quilt is basted. Release the tape and check the back of the quilt to make sure no wrinkles have formed, and only then close all those pins. Trust me: you don't want to close the pins only to discover you need to reopen and redo a section!

If you are working on a carpeted floor, you can use "T" pins to secure the backing, then proceed as above. Be sure not to catch the carpet fibers in the safety pins, or you'll baste your quilt to the carpet and end up with carpet fuzz quilted onto the back of the quilt! Erg!

For quilts that are larger than the table top, I do one corner at a time, clamping the backing, smoothing out the layers, pinning, checking for smoothness, and closing the pins. Then I shift the quilt so a neighboring segment or corner is on the surface of the table and pin baste that section. I continue working on sections until the entire quilt is basted.

Marginalia: I quilt from the center out. If my quilt is on the large side, when I approach the outer edges, I will check to see if I need to readjust the pin basting. During the quilting process, sometimes the backing fabric eases and migrates a bit and the outer edges need to be smoothed out.

ALTERNATIVES TO PIN BASTING

Spray basting: Basting spray is a wonderful invention, provided you use a light hand! This has become my favorite way to baste all small wall quilts and most large quilts as well. In all cases, follow the instructions on the can. Be aware that basting spray migrates on unseen air currents. If you have asthma or other breathing difficulties, this may not be a viable option for you. Always spray baste in a well-ventilated area with no cross-breezes.

Water-soluble thread: You can pin baste more lightly and stabilize the quilt by machine basting with water-soluble thread. Do *not* do this during high humidity season since the moisture in the air could weaken or cause the thread to dissolve! Some folks will use this thread in both bobbin and needle. Others use it as the bobbin thread, with a fine poly, monofilament, or cotton in the top. Most manufacturers recommend using it only in the bobbin (less potential for evaporation into the innards of your machine). Be sure to safety pin the corners to prevent the backing from coming loose.

Small swatch misted, and water-soluble thread basting partially removed

Fusible batting: Oh WOW do I love this stuff! Maybe even more than basting spray! When the batting comes out of the bag, it is sort of stuck to itself. Gently unfold it and smooth it out. Follow the instructions on the package for adhering.

Fusible web: Here's a radical concept: Fuse your entire top (and maybe the back!) to the batting. For A Sense of Place: The Wall, I pinned batting several inches larger than the intended finished size of the quilt to my design wall. I pinned pre-fused sky fabrics to the batting until I was pleased with the arrangement. I then fused the sky pieces in place with the iron right there on the design wall. I continued working this way until the composition was complete, then I moved the quilt to my ironing board and ironed again. I spray basted the backing fabric and was ready to quilt!

You can also use what I call the Confetti Method of basting with fusible web: cut bits of fusible web into small squares and scatter them across the batting. Layer the backing onto the batting and iron it in place.

A Sense of Place: The Wall, detail

A Sense of Place: The Wall, 30" x 27", made by the author.

Setting Up for Machine Quilting

If your sewing room is like mine, any horizontal surface quickly ends up filled with something. *Move* that stuff off the sewing table so you have open space to manage the bulk of the quilt. Create as large, flat, and smooth a surface as you can to support the quilt.

If your sewing surface is smooth and clean, it will be easier to maneuver the quilt. Try polishing your work surface with car wax, furniture polish (in either case make sure it won't stain the fabric), silicone spray (be sure to cover the machine first), or one of the Teflon® "slip and slide" materials. Some quilters spray starch the backing fabric to help it slide more easily when free-motion quilting.

Starting and Stopping
PULL THE THREAD TO THE TOP

To avoid ugly thread nests on the underside of your quilt, first pull your bobbin thread to the top of your project. Take one stitch or hand-walk the needle one stitch. Give the needle thread a tug to pull the bobbin thread to the top and fish out the tail of the bobbin thread. Hold both tails to the side and start quilting.

For a quick start and stop, take several tiny stitches in the first (or last) quarter inch of quilting, then *carefully* trim the tails. This works best with cotton thread.

With poly or nylon threads, tiny starting and stopping stitches can sometimes come undone or fray. With these threads, you'll want to use an heirloom quality finish. After bringing the bobbin thread to the top, make sure you have about 3"–5" of thread from the needle and the bobbin, then begin quilting without the short stitches. When you complete the line of stitching, give yourself about 3"–5" of thread before clipping the tails.

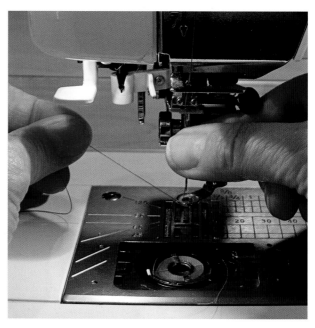

I often pinch the top thread against the needle to make it easier to get the bobbin thread to pop up to the top.

Pull ALL of the threads to the back of the quilt. Knot the top and bobbin threads with a square knot right next to where the needle thread comes out of the back of the quilt. Thread a regular needle (or use an easy self-threading needle and snap the tails in) and poke it into the hole from which the top thread exits the back. Bury the thread and knot in the batting. If your knot is reluctant to pass back into the inside of the quilt, give a gentle tug on the thread and scrape over the knot area with your fingernail to encourage it to pop inside.

Hint: I have an irrational fear that I will snip a hole in the quilt when trimming the thread tails. Here's how to avoid that. In one hand, hold the scissors slightly open but don't move the blades! In the other hand, hold the thread tails near the end. Pull up so the quilt lifts off the table. Holding the scissors steady near the surface of the quilt, pull the thread tails into the notch of the scissor blades, which will cut them. The thread will retract under the quilt backing once the tails are clipped.

Close-up of short stitches, from top to bottom:

1. Using stop lockstitch at both ends, 2.5 stitch length, tails not trimmed

2. Using stop/lockstitch at both ends, 2.5 stitch length, tails trimmed

3. Stitches at 0 length, 5 stitches a 1.0 length, 2.5 quilting (and repeat at end), untrimmed

4. Same as 3, tails trimmed

5. No lock stitches at all, just 2.5 stitch length, untrimmed

Like Driving a Car

When you free-motion stitch or quilt, you need to coordinate three things: your eyes (look where you are going); your hands (the steering wheel or the quilt); and your foot (the gas or power pedal). At first, free-motion stitching will seem at least as awkward as driving did way back when you first learned, but give yourself permission to be a beginner!

The bottom line of quilting is as stitched, with tails dangling. The middle line shows the bobbin thread pulled to the top (normally I'd do this on the back, but for the illustration, it is on the top) with the two threads knotted and slipped into a easy threading needle. The needle is inserted into the hole for the final stitch. The top line shows a perfect end to the line of stitching; the tails have been pulled back to the top of the quilt, just to the right of the line of quilting.

Tip

An easy threading needle is great for cottons and many poly threads but it can break metallic, holographic, and some rayon and poly threads. For those, use a crewel needle or other large-eyed needle.

STITCHES: EVEN, UNEVEN, IT'S UP TO YOU!

Stitch length: In traditional hand quilting, an even stitch length is prized, as it is in most machine quilting. What you *really* want to be able to do is practice and develop the skill to create the stitch length you want *when* you want it.

With free motion, you control the length of the stitch. It's like Goldilocks again. You want stitches that are "just right" for you and your project.

Remember the impact a given thread will have on stitch appearance when contemplating stitch length.

Stitch length affects the appearance of the thread, especially shiny ones. A shorter stitch length casts more shadows on the sheen of the shiny threads and mutes it somewhat. If you want a lot of glitz, use a longer stitch length.

Picture of two curls: in the two curls in the top right corner, the larger/left curl is made with longer stitches; it is impossible to turn a tight curve with longer stitches; the second curl has much shorter stitches at the tip, permitting a tighter curve.

I used six threads in this gold-on-blue stitch-out. Left to right:

The Bottom Line, 60-wt. poly, shiny

Mettler Silk-finish 50-wt. cotton, matte

Sulky 40-wt. rayon, shiny

Superior Threads 40-wt. trilobal poly, shiny

Superior Threads Metallic, shiny

Superior Threads Glitter, very shiny

By changing the stitch length from 4.0 (long) to 3.0, 2.0, and finally 1.0 (very short) I was able to mute the shininess of the thread, as you can see at the top of the photo to the right.

Heresy warning: Do you want all your stitches the same length? I don't! One of the beauties of machine quilting is being able to make tiny curls and bends. For these short curves to be smooth, you need a shorter stitch length. With practice, you will develop a rhythm of free-motion stitching that is comfortable and creates a consistent length on the straightaway with a shorter stitch length on the tight curves.

Even more heretically, you may want highly irregular stitch length on art quilts to create a look or effect. You can use irregular stitch length to your advantage; just make sure it looks like you have done it on purpose.

POSTCARD FROM RAJAHSTAN, 40" x 49", made by Rana O'Connor, Portland, Maine. Rana's quilt of a man and his horse perfectly illustrates the use of different stitch lengths to achieve a special effect...in this case, the long hairs on the horse's muzzle (see the detail below).

POSTCARD FROM RAJAHSTAN, detail

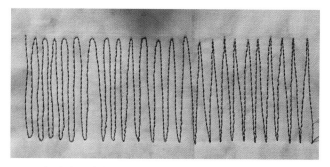

On the left, I didn't pause as I changed directions; in the center, I paused, but for a nano-second or less. On the right, where the points are sharp and crisp, I paused. However, you have to be careful not to stop too long, or you'll end up with an "acorn"—a nubbin of thread knotted on the back.

Looking ahead as I stitch works for me on open spaces up to about 2½"–3" long. Longer than that and my line tends to wobble.

SPEED

How fast or slow you quilt is a personal decision. You do want to strive for a consistent speed as this will help you create a consistently even stitch or consistently even increases and decreases in stitching those curves.

Many newer machines have speed regulators that permit you to set the maximum needle speed to ⅓ or ½ of full speed. Then you can "floor" the foot pedal, yet still maintain the slower speed.

As you practice (yep, the dreaded "P" word again!), you will find that some quilting motions such as stippling or making small bubbles require a faster needle speed, while you need a slower speed for precise placement of stitches, such as on a feathered wreath or when contouring a face.

SHARP POINTS

Just as you adjust your stitching to create small, smooth curves, on pointed designs, pause just half a heartbeat at the point to get a crisp, sharp result.

LOOKING DOWN THE ROAD

When driving a car you look down the road, not at the hood ornament. Do the same thing with your quilting. Here's an exercise I teach in all my classes:

- Draw a grid of lines 1" apart.
- Starting in one corner, aim for the next intersection of the lines.
- As you approach the intersection, shift your eyes ahead to the next one.

It's like magic! Even though you aren't looking at that first intersection, the needle will stitch right through it.

DON'T DRIVE YOURSELF INTO A CORNER

When you're going somewhere, you plan your route to avoid dead ends and one-way streets that go in the wrong direction. Do the same thing with your quilting. Before quilting a design, think ahead about the route you will take as you stitch. Trace around the design with your finger without lifting it or use a wet-erase marker on an acetate overlay (see page 89). OR use a pencil on paper or make a photocopy of your quilting pattern, slip it inside a plastic bag or a clear plastic page protector, and use a wash-away marker to trace over the designs. Your hands will become familiar with the movements needed to create the shape; it will then become easier to repeat those shapes when free-motion quilting. Tracing like this will help you internalize the pathway you will take at the sewing machine.

If you are outline quilting a design on a border, study the design to see what order and direction to stitch so that you don't quilt yourself into a place where you have to make unnecessary stops and starts.

PRACTICE BEFORE QUILTING

Try quilting your name! Watch a child concentrate so *hard* to make the shapes of letters when learning to write. As adults, we have completely internalized that process. It's much the same with quilting: in the beginning you *really* need to think how to make the shapes, but soon, it will become second nature.

Try quilting your doodles... you know, those marks and drawings on the edges of grocery lists and whatnot. Look at them and think how you might turn your own shapes into quilting designs.

Some folks find geometric and straight-line designs more comfortable, others gravitate to circular or undulating shapes. Try both. When you are new to free-motion quilting, go with what feels most comfortable and build up your skills and confidence. After a while, challenge yourself to do a design that is "not you," and build up those skills. It's that practice thing—the more you do it, the easier it gets!

PLAN YOUR PAUSES

Because your arms are only so long, you have to reposition your hands. ALWAYS make sure both the sewing machine and the movement of the quilt have come to **a full and complete stop** before you move your hands. If either or both of these movements is still going on, you will get "jogs" that interrupt the stitching line.

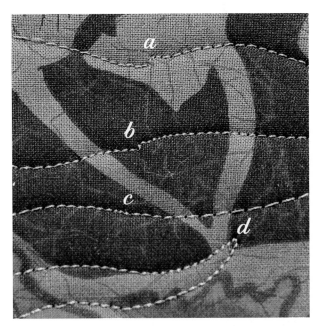

You want the places where you pause to reposition your hands to be unnoticeable when the quilting is done. To help disguise any wobbles, plan your stops for a place on the surface where the thread color matches the fabric (a) instead of where it contrasts (b). If you are using a variegated thread, you need to guess ahead to where the thread color will blend with the background, but it can be done! It is possible to have smooth, even starts in the middle of a very long straightaway (c), but it takes practice. You can also minimize the risk of uneven lines and wobbles by choosing to pause and reposition your hands where the free-motion stitching changes directions at a point (d).

*The top third is quilted in every other square, making it balanced.

*The middle third is quilted in every square, making it balanced and dense.

*The lower third is quilted in one of every six squares. Compared to the other two sections, it is uneven, although if the entire quilt was done this way, it could be considered balanced.

Most teachers, including me, recommend that you have your needle in the *down* position when you stop. (Be sure to "puddle" the quilt into hills and valleys around the needle to take the weight of the quilt off the needle and make maneuvering it easier.) Some folks, including some major award-winning quilters, prefer to stop with the needle up. Try both ways and see what works best for you.

STITCHING DENSITY

Aesthetically, how much quilting is enough or too much is a personal choice, though practical factors do apply. I love densely stitched quilts where the thread adds another layer of design. However, some folks think this is too much and prefer a softer, more open look.

An additional factor in determining density is the batting you choose. The reason quilters of the past quilted so closely was to keep the cotton fibers evenly distributed across the quilt. You know what happens if you accidentally leave a tissue in a pocket and it goes through the wash. Without crosshatching and dense quilting, the same thing would have happened to the cotton batting of old. Check your batting package to see how close or far apart you can quilt the batting you have chosen.

If you want a flat quilt, the distribution of the stitching needs to be fairly even to prevent rippling and unwanted bulges. If one area is densely stitched and the rest is not, you will introduce distortion because stitched areas will "draw up" and "shrink" the quilt compared to the lightly stitched areas.

Troubleshooting

❧ If you have a *molehill* in the body of a quilt, you can try to add more quilting to "shrink up" that area.

❧ If you have *rippled outside edges* of the quilt, you have two choices. Sometimes the ripples are due to what I call the "I'm tired of quilting and want this done" syndrome. By the time we make it to the edge, we just don't want to put in the time to quilt the borders as densely as the center. The solution in this instance is to do the extra quilting.

❧ Sometimes the cause of the rippling isn't so easily diagnosed. As a solution, you can run a long machine-basting stitch (4.0 or 5.0 length) at the very edge of the quilt where it will be covered by the finish treatment and ease or gently gather in the excess. Pin your binding/edge finish onto the slightly gathered edge and stitch, being careful not to sew any puckers or tucks into the surface or backing.

Quilting Design

This may be my all time favorite part of all quilting: designing and executing the quilting design. There have been many volumes written on design, on quilting designs, and creativity, so although we can't cover everything here, I can show you some of my tips, tricks, and favorite things.

You can break any design down into simple components. Just as words are composed of groups of letters, designs are made up of basic shapes and elements.

My "light bulb moment" came in a class with master artist, photographer, and quilter Hollis Chatelain. She asked us to imagine an ant with inky feet walking across our arm, and visualize the tracks it would leave behind. These lines are contour lines, just like on a topographical map showing elevation changes, and they become your stitching lines. If a small army of ants walked up the tree one inch apart, the lines would appear closer together on the edges of the tree; the different spaces between the lines gives an impression of roundness. Or the ant could spiral around the tree trunk.

How to Block a Quilt

Sometimes, despite your best efforts to have a quilt lie flat, it won't. All is not lost! You can remedy the situation just like you would wrinkles in a pair of wool pants or wonky knitting: moisture. You will need a flat space where you can lay out the entire quilt.

Secure the quilt to the surface so the edges are where you want them. Use a spray bottle with water or a steam iron to moisten (but not soak) the quilt. Flatten the quilt with your hand. Allow the quilt to dry COMPLETELY. This may take several days. When you move the quilt, be careful not to stretch out the "fiddly" parts!

BLUE MEN, 78" x 58", made by Hollis Chatelain. In the detail photo, you can see how Hollis chose to use subtle gradations of color and contour to create the shapes of the face and turban.

BLUE MEN, detail

Using nested, curved zigzags will also create the impression of shape, but going in a different direction. If you use three colors of thread instead of one, you get further shape and definition. Hollis Chatelain is a master of using thread to create contours and shading. BLUE MEN is a wholecloth quilt she painted in shades of blue dye. Any and ALL other colors that you see come entirely from the thread she selected for the stitching.

CONTRAST IN LINE

One of the ironies of quilting—particularly in traditional quilting—is that with all the attention given to creating the line and perfecting the stitch, it is actually the spaces between the lines that catch our attention—the shapes created by the lines!

In quilting designs, contrast in the shapes of the lines and density of the quilting will allow some areas to come forward and others to recede. Let's take a closer look at the wreath sampler. The central motif is more obvious when the scale of the background quilting is either much smaller or larger than the motif itself.

This sampler shows a traditional wreath with a variety of background fill patterns. The wreaths in the top row are quilted with 40-wt. Superior Thread polyesters in colors that match the hand-dyed fabric; the bottom row is quilted with a darker color. It is interesting to note how much more visible some wreaths are.

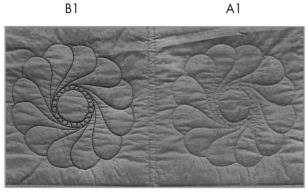

In the wreaths B1 and A1, there is no background quilting at all. A1 is quilted with matching thread, B1 with darker colored thread. In a show, a quilt with A1 blocks would probably receive "needs more quilting" comments, as the background is a bit ripply.

As I discovered while making this teaching sampler, it is very good to test-drive your threads. The darker thread is fine on the feathers on the left-side wreath B2, but too dark for my taste in the small pearls in the center.

A3   A4

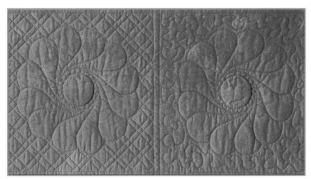

B4   A4

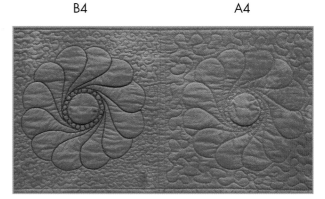

The A3 background is the small grid; A4 is a meandering pattern that creates spaces about the same size as the grid. However, because the background is a series of curved lines (I think of jigsaw puzzle pieces when I'm doing it: two innies, two outies; one innie, three outies, and so on), the contrast with the curved lines in the wreath isn't very effective.

By decreasing the size of the meander to a stipple, the wreath is suddenly much more visible (and, in this case, it isn't because of the change in thread color on the wreath).

B3   B4

LEFT: Finally, compare the small grid and the small stipple. Both are effective at creating contrast and bringing attention to all that hard work, making a lovely wreath.

A dense quilting pattern in the background makes it recede. This is something I didn't know when I started hand quilting a queen-sized Mariner's Compass, OCEANS ALIVE. (It was the second quilt I began but it took a decade to finish quilting it, hence my devotion to machine quilting.) I wanted to define the light and dark areas on the orca whales, so I stippled the light areas. It would have been better if I had simply outlined the areas on the whales, then stippled densely in the space just around them to make the orcas pop.

RIGHT: In this teaching sampler for some free-motion fill patterns, I used straight lines to define areas, then quilted the spaces created with alternating straight-line and curved-line motifs. I made sure to leave some areas unquilted to create visual patterns in the designs.

The sun has spirals in the center and flames on the edges, and though both are curved lines, the points on the flame tips cause them to read more as a straight design (and the line of straight stitching to define the circle of the sun helps, too). Within the rays coming off the snail/wave arc, you can see various fill patterns, but they, too, alternate between predominantly straight-line designs and predominantly curvy shapes. Finally, color changes in the threads add an additional subtle bit of contrast.

I alternated straight lines to create a diamond-shaped "woven" grid. The snails/waves alternate between smooth and spiked and the surface of the moon has large craters and small ridges.

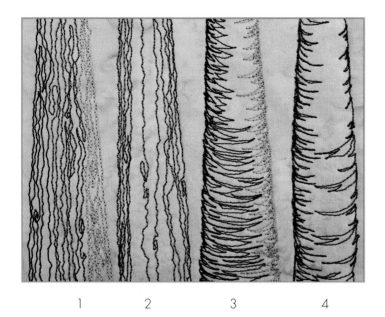

1   2   3   4

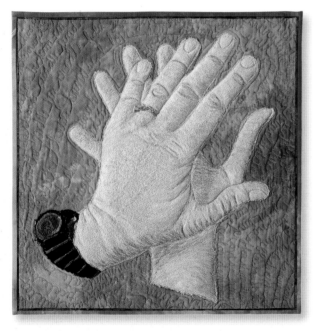

WITH THESE HANDS, 12" x 12", made by the author.
For indoor or abstract pieces, pick a single spot to be your
light source to give a coherent feel to your piece. Here the
light source is from the upper left corner. This means the
top left-hand side of the hands is lightest, while the right
side of the fingers and hands are darkest. I used fourteen
colors of beige and pink cotton threads plus a gray and
pool blue for the veins to create this thread appliqué.

PICK A LIGHT SOURCE

Art quilters as well as traditional appliquérs need to think about a light source, especially when working with representative pieces. In landscapes, the sun is the usual light source. If the light comes in low from the side, it casts long shadows denoting early morning or late afternoon. You will be able to create more realistic imagery by defining a light source and using a gradation of light to dark threads for shading and highlighting your shapes.

In the tree trunk sample, tree trunks 2 and 4 are done with medium green thread only, with density of stitching used to convey light direction and shape. By varying the spacing on trunk 2, it gives the illusion of a cylindrical shape. Trunks 1 and 3 are made with three shades of green. Trunk 1 simulates a bark pattern, while trunk 3 uses nested, curved V shapes to imply contour. You can nest all the way across the span of the trunk (on the bottom) or leave an unquilted space (the top). In this sample, the light comes from the right.

Fingers are cylinders, just like tree trunks, so I free-motion nested zigzags to create the shading on the fingers. See the larger photo of WITH THESE HANDS on page 43. First, I selected my lightest color and used straight stitch zigzags to shape the left side of my fingers.

Second, I switched to a dark thread to make the shadowy sections underneath and to the right. I then filled in the middle with 3-5 values ranging from medium dark to medium to medium light. The darkest colored threads were reserved for the shadows created by the creases in my hands, the shadowed area on the palm of my right hand, and underneath my left thumb and wrist, but I still used a range of thread colors from medium dark to deepest dark.

The year after my dad died, my mom returned to Japan where she lived in 1946–47, working with the US occupying military forces. She had fallen in love with the country and the people back then and always wanted to return. She invited me to go with her in 1996. In 2002, my skills were finally up to the challenge of interpreting a photo that I took on that trip.

ALMS, 24" x 30", made by the author

ALMS, detail. I had to interpret a range of flat, smooth surfaces in quilting, yet differentiate between sidewalk, smooth stone, bumpy stone, glass, painted plywood, board and batten, stone pillar, cloth banner, and cloth. I took artistic license and changed the paved street into cobblestones!

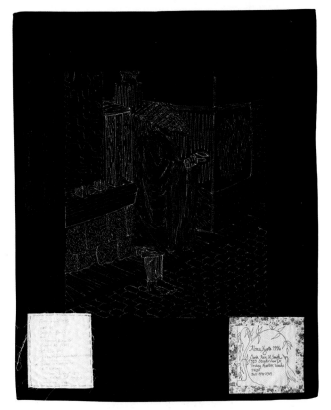

ALMS. The back clearly shows the wide range of free-motion patterns I used for these smooth-ish surfaces. I chose to use a bobbin thread that blended with my needle thread, which gave me a wonderful line drawing on the back. Be aware that some judges in quilt shows don't like this effect, but that's OK. I love it so I'm going to do it the way I like!

Cindy Sissler Simms sent Mariner's Compass blocks to my two sons. I quilted the blocks and made them into pillows. Because the quilting on their bed quilts is fairly simple, I wanted to keep the look on these Mariner's Compass blocks clean and simple, too. I used straight lines only; the first line of quilting is the distance from the edge of the presser foot, run along the edge of the piece. Then I stitched a parallel line, again running the edge of the presser foot along the first line of quilting, but moving the needle closer to the previous stitching. The contrast in the width of the channels gives the design interest.

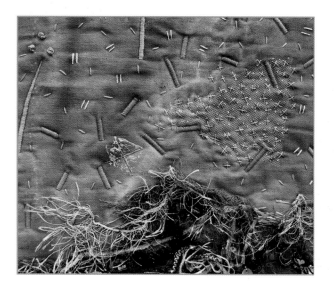

FEED DOGS UP: STRAIGHT LINE DESIGNS

You can also achieve contrast in quilting that is done exclusively with the walking foot instead of free motion. You may have physical limitations that make it hard for you to free motion, or you may be a total beginner and this is a great place to start. (When I started machine quilting I didn't know you shouldn't use an ultra thick batt, let alone what a walking foot was!) Maybe you just want to do something fairly simple and straightforward. You can do just that and get beautiful results using simple patterns and colorful threads.

With the walking foot, or an integrated even feed mechanism, you can easily make straight, even lines and gently curving lines. Tight curves are harder, requiring a fair amount of starting, stopping, pivoting, and so on. To minimize the amount of starting/stopping/turning, and the attendant rearranging of the bulk of the quilt, you'll want to plan your quilting design to take advantage of these strengths and avoid weaknesses.

WHAT ROLE DO YOU WANT YOUR QUILTING TO PLAY?

Only you can decide what look is right for you, but if you understand the principle of contrast, you'll be able to better achieve your quilting goals. How dominant do you want your quilting to be, or do you want it to be secondary to the overall design? If the latter, you may want all the quilting patterns (or the only pattern) to be of similar size across the quilt surface.

LEFT: SEA BOTTOM BLUES, detail, made by Kathy Daniels. Kathy often uses chunks of satin stitching interspersed across a surface the way one would embroider a piece, and also uses tapered bits that look like blades of grass. This detail shows how effectively hand and machine stitching can be combined. I need to do this!

RIGHT: SEA BOTTOM BLUES, 15½" x 38", made by Kathy Daniels, China Village, Maine

TEA, 19" x 16", made by the author. In TEA I quilted the entire piece densely; the quilting plays a subordinate role to the color of my breakfast dishes and book.

TEA, detail below. I quilted simple contour lines about ⅛" to ¹⁄₁₆" apart that follow the shapes of the objects. The thread colors accentuate the colors of the fabrics. The background quilting is in a fan shape similar to the stucco walls in my grandma's kitchen and is less dense. Stitching lines about ¼" apart flatten the background. There are no "relief" or puffy areas and the quilting is secondary to the imagery and color.

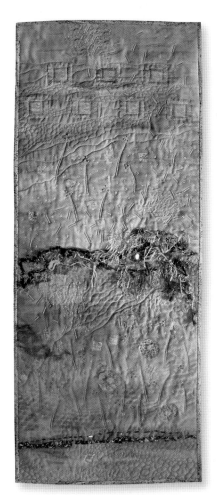

If you want the quilting to play a highly visible role in the quilt, you will want to heighten the contrast in the various quilting motifs and patterns using both value (light versus dark); color (matching versus not); scale (large versus small motifs); and shape (straight versus curved lines). If you are auditioning a quilting pattern and it doesn't seem quite right, ask yourself: is there enough contrast? Are all my lines straight? Are the shapes created by the lines the same size or do they vary?

Marginalia: Remember, you can use the color of thread to help "improve" the contrast of your appliqués! If you find that you have too much contrast, soften it with a lighter color quilting thread. If not enough contrast, use a darker color.

When Pamela Allen transitioned from being a successful studio artist using fairly traditional media to being a successful art quilter, she came with an arsenal of imagery and a well-developed personal style. In addition to the immediate impact of her quirky imagery, she uses an inspiring array of designs in her background quilting.

Look again at the front of COLD CANADIANS and pick out all those fun designs. For me, this type of quilting represents the best art quilting—the visual impact from a distance grabs you and makes you come closer to see, and when you get closer, there is so much more to reward you!

COLD CANADIANS, 33" x 47", made by Pamela Allen. In COLD CANADIANS, you can enjoy the embellishments and then notice the quilting.

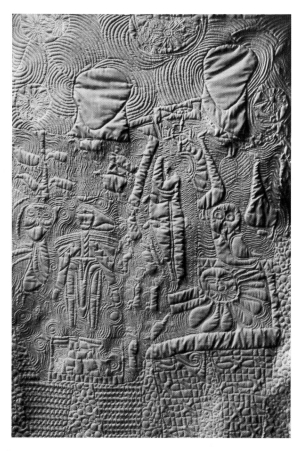

COLD CANADIANS, detail. It is when you look at the back of the quilt that you realize how much fun Pamela had quilting the piece!

IF YOU GIVE A MAN A FISH
YOU FEED HIM FOR A DAY
IF YOU TEACH A MAN TO FISH
YOU FEED HIM FOR A LIFETIME

TEACH A MAN TO FISH, 36" x 69", made by Pat LaPierre. Pat used small fill patterns on the fish. By combining components quilted separately, she was able to create stunning dimension in her quilt, and alternate more open quilting in the sign with varied but dense designs on the fish.

TEACH A MAN TO FISH, detail

MOON OVER THE MOUNTAIN, 8½" x 11", made by the author. In my June 2006 journal quilt, the densely quilted areas alternate with more lightly quilted sections. Variety and contrast in the shapes of the lines tell part of the story.

The hills in the foreground are quilted with long straight lines in alternating directions, while the distant mountains are quilted with craggy, bending ridges. The moon alternates between craters and ridgelines, while the sky is filled with swirls.

MOSSY SHADOWS, 9½"-14" x 34", made by Deborah Boschert, Lewisville, Texas. In this quilt from her Anthony Avenue series, Deborah uses similar motifs in her quilting. The quilting patterns cascade down the quilt in bands, each stitched in a different color. Here the quilting plays an important role in the overall impression of the quilt, without dominating or receding into a supporting role.

Working Out the Design

The easiest way to work out your quilting designs is right on the quilt! You can do this using a clear overlay or tracing paper. For the first rounds of drafting and sketching out, I prefer a clear acetate sheet (available from an art supply store or online). Some folks prefer "quilters' vinyl" or a clear shower curtain. I find that these plastics ripple some and the surface distortions bother me. Use what works for you!

To avoid accidentally marking the quilt or having ink transfer from the overlay sheet to the top, tape over the edges with masking or painter's tape. Mark one side "This side UP" in Sharpie or other permanent marker, then use that side ONLY for sketching out your designs.

I use two of the acetate sheets to try different designs in each corner, or set them next to each other for larger designs. Using a digital camera to record "possibles" is a good habit to develop.

You can also take a digital photo of your quilt, print it out or display it on your computer screen, then place a clear page protector over it, and test drive design ideas. This works well for bed-sized quilts.

A Closing Thought

I can think of nothing better to sum up threadwork than to repeat words uttered nearly 450 years ago, at about the age of 80.

"I am still learning."

Michelangelo Buonarroti

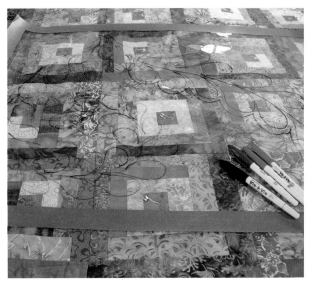

Here I'm trying a feathered wreath on the diagonals of this Log Cabin. I used a 24" x 40" sheet of acetate and wet-erase markers designed for use on overhead transparencies (available at office supply stores). The dry erase markers smudge too easily and can end up on your top (yuck!). The wet-erase markers wipe off with a damp paper towel and come in red, green, blue, and black—colors that can be seen on most quilt tops. When I'm done for the day, I rinse off the acetate sheet under the shower and drape it over the shower rod to dry.

MOSSY SHADOWS, detail. This detail photo shows Deborah's use of different thread colors and different quilting patterns to create the meandering pathways down the face of the quilt.

Nearly No-Mark Free-Motion Quilting Sampler

18" x 18", made by the author

TECHNIQUES: *free-motion quilting*

This sampler is one I developed for my first free-motion machine quilting class. All of the designs were chosen from motifs that I use regularly. I particularly love designs from Mother Nature: I figure if she never made two leaves exactly alike, I don't have to either!

Here's a chance to practice both straight-line and undulating shapes. When you are new to free-motion quilting, go with what feels most comfortable to build up your skills and confidence. After a while, challenge yourself to do designs that are "not you." It's that old practice thing: the more you do it, the easier it gets!

Fabrics and Notions

- ⅝ yard white or very light solid/nearly solid fabric for the top and backing
- ¼ yard for binding
- 22" x 22" batting
- Marking pen or pencil of your choice
- Rotary ruler, at least 3" x 14"
- 2 colors of contrasting thread for the top
- Matching thread for background quilting in the border
- Matching thread for the back to use in the bobbin, may be the same weight as the top thread or a lighter-weight bobbin thread

Finger press a crease in the center *vertically*

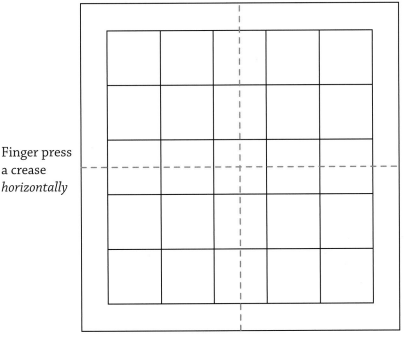

Finger press a crease *horizontally*

Mark a 5 x 5 grid of squares, with lines 2½" apart.

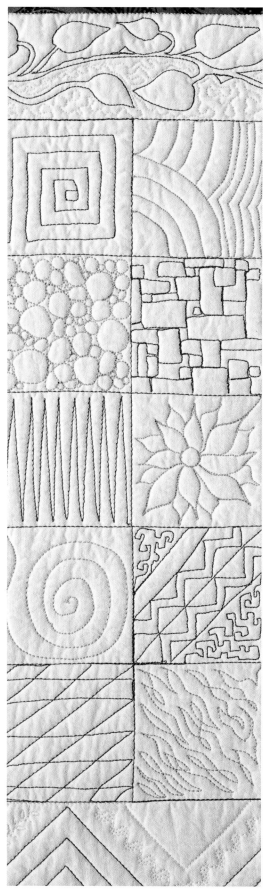

Making the Sampler

Fold an 18" x 18" square of fabric horizontally, finger pressing a crease at the center. Draw a 12½" long line 1¼" from the crease, then two more lines 2½" apart. Repeat on the other side of the center crease. Repeat vertically, creating a 5 x 5 grid of 2½" squares.

Layer the top with 22" x 22" squares of batting and backing; use basting spray or pin baste with safety pins.

Stitch over the grid lines with contrasting thread.

The no-mark quilt patterns (pages 93-94) are labeled to indicate where to start (•); the stitching path (→); and where to stop (■).

Stitch straight-line patterns in magenta and curvy designs in lime green to form an overall checkerboard design.

Begin the free-motion quilting in the center square; this forward-backward zigzag pattern is most similar to the motions you are used to making when sewing with the feed dogs engaged.

Next, try the side-to-side "nested" zigzags; this is a wonderful movement to create depth, shading, and contouring. (See detail photos of Bigajos Warrior and Blue Men, pages 44 and 78, for ways to use nested zigzags.)

Continue on, filling the squares with different patterns, using my designs or trying some of your own.

Use a combination of magenta and lime threads in the borders. Quilt the bottom border using a walking foot and both straight and decorative stitching. Quilt the side borders with free-motion designs.

Select thread that matches the fabric to "pop" the border quilting designs. On the double feathered arrow, I used two lines of narrow echo quilting. For the top and left borders, I left the outside edge unquilted but compressed the inside edge with both traditional stippling and a simple zigzag, which achieves the same relief effect as stippling. Decide which look you prefer for *your* quilting!

Trim the completed top to 18" x 18".

Cut 2 straight-grain binding strips 1½" wide and join. Stitch the binding to the front of the top using a ¼" seam allowance. Turn to the back, fold under the edge, and hand-stitch in place.

Sit back and enjoy your piece, share it with friends, and celebrate with chocolate!

● START ——→ follow the arrows ■ END

• START → follow the arrows ■ END

Sarah Ann Smith © 2005

First Frost Table Runner

14" x 57", made by the author

TECHNIQUES: *leaf printing, free-motion quilting, couching in the ditch*

Fabrics and Supplies

- ✤ 2¼ yards hand-dyed or batik "solid" in a pale, wintry blue
- ✤ 19" x 64" batting
- ✤ Assorted decorative threads; I used:
  - Yenmet Gold, PH-110
  - Superior Metallics™ silver 64
  - Superior Rainbows™ blue/teal variegated 831
  - Superior Metallics gold N116
  - Superior Metallics variegated gold 25
  - Superior Highlights 709, Caribbean blue
  - Superior Nature Colors™ 70, cerulean blue
  - Superior Glitter™ opal, a frosty pale white/pink/blue
  - Sew-Art Invisible Nylon
- ✤ Textile paints; I used:
  - Lumiere in metallic gold, pearl turquoise, and silver
  - Pebeo Setacolor Shimmer electric blue 69 and shimmer pearl
  - Stewart Gill Byzantia in Aegean
  - Jacquard Textile Color™ opaque white
- ✤ Sponge roller or sponge paintbrush
- ✤ Soft rubber brayer (like a small paint roller but a bit more firm)
- ✤ 8" x 10" glass, edges taped, or a plastic page protector as a palette
- ✤ An assortment of leaves, clean and dry
- ✤ Paper towels, parchment, or other paper
- ✤ Plastic to cover your work surface
- ✤ Lightly padded surface/worktable

Leaf Printing How-To

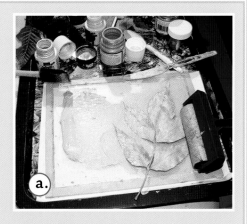

a.

↬ Lay fabric to be printed onto a plastic-covered, lightly padded work surface.

↬ Squeeze or pour paint onto the glass palette.

↬ Roll with the sponge roller to create an even coating on the roller (a).

b.

↬ Place the leaf bottom-side-up on clean/dry plastic or glass palette and coat with paint using the roller.

↬ Lift the leaf and place it paint-side-down onto the fabric (b).

↬ Place parchment or other paper over the leaf.

c.

↬ Roll over the leaf with a clean, soft rubber brayer OR press with your hands. The amount of pressure applied with a roller versus your hands differs. A brayer will produce a finer, lighter print. If the contrast between paint and fabric is too subtle, add more paint or try pressing the leaf onto the surface with your hands (c).

↬ Remove the paper and carefully lift up the leaf.

d.

↬ Allow the paint to dry and heat-set or cure it according to the paint manufacturer's instructions (d).

Cut a 33" x 65" piece of the background fabric.

Print leaves onto the fabric, allow to dry, and set according to the paint manufacturer's instructions. I used two colors and diluted each with white to get two lighter shades.

Cut two lengths from the printed fabric, 16" x 60" for the top and 20" x 64" for the back, selecting the portion you like best for the top. Layer with the batting and prepare for quilting. If you pin baste, be careful not to pin through the paint.

Decide which threads to use on which leaves. Make sure that your selections will scatter the colors of thread across the surface of the quilt.

Hint: Test drive the threads and colors in the corners. They will be cut off, so they are the perfect spots to make a visual decision visually (remember this?).

Quilt the printed leaves. Quilt leaf shapes to fill the background. Use the leaves as templates for the background quilting, tracing around the edges and marking a center vein. Tie off/bury any thread tails.

Trim the runner so that the long sides are straight and parallel. A 20½" square ruler makes this quite easy. If you don't have such a large ruler, use a marking pen to mark the edges first, then trim after you are sure the lines are straight, even, and parallel along the entire length.

Square off the short ends, making sure your corners are exactly 90 degrees.

Find and mark the exact center of the short sides. Using your rotary-cutting ruler, mark two 45-degree diagonal lines from the center point at both ends of the runner.

Cut off the corners along the marked lines.

Cut enough 2¼" strips from the remaining fabric to make approximately 160" of binding. Fold in half lengthwise, wrong-sides together, and press.

Apply the binding to the BACK of the table runner. Turn the binding to the front and stitch down by machine using a narrow zigzag, blind hem, or blanket stitch. Couch gold yarn or cording in the ditch, next to the binding.

Mountain Seasons

12½" x 27", made by the author

TECHNIQUES: *fusible appliqué, free-motion embroidery, fabric painting with freezer-paper stencils, couching yarn edges on windows*

Fabrics and Supplies

- ¼ yard Timtex®, Pellon® Peltex, or similar stiff interfacing for the windows (The windows are made the same way as fabric postcards.)
- ½ yard fusible web
- Assorted scraps of cottons and silk:
    blue for the sky and bay
    greens and browns for the mountain and hills (Use more detailed prints in the foreground, and plainer, mottled pieces for the distant hills.)
    browns, and gray/brown, or green/brown batiks for the branches
    two pinks for spring flowers *(supplies continued)*

- 4 pieces of "Why did I buy this?" window backing 4½" x 6 ½" *(It won't show but you need backing because the windows tend to curl when they have fabric on only one side of the stiffener.)*
- ¾ yard for background and facing strips
- ¾ yard for backing and sleeve (I made my windows first, checked my stash, then took my windows with me to the store to audition fabrics.)
- 4 lengths of thick yarn 25"–30" (I used Lion Brand® Lion® Suede yarn in dark brown.)
- Threads to match your fabrics; I used:
  - Superior Rainbows™ Bubble Gum for the petals and buds
  - Superior Glitter™ Pearl, for ice on winter branches
  - Rusts and oranges, solids and/or variegated to stitch the fall leaves
  - Assorted greens and variegated greens in 40-wt. trilobal polyesters (the nice shiny ones!) for the spring and summer leaves
- 16½" x 31" batting
- Jacquard Textile Color opaque white
- 1"–2" sponge brush, stencil brush, or sponge
- Freezer paper
- X-Acto® knife and paper scissors

Making the Windows

Cut 4 pieces of Peltex or similar stabilizer 4" x 6" for your window bases.

Prepare your fabrics for fusible appliqué by applying fusible web to the wrong side.

Cut 4 pieces 4½" x 4½" from your prepared sky fabric. Fuse to the top of the stabilizer.

Free-cut the remaining appliqué pieces using the photographs as a guide. Add an extra ¼" along the bottom of each to prevent any gaps when positioning them on the bases. (A full pattern of all four seasons is available for download from my Web site. See Resources, page 109.)

Hint: When making the wallhanging, be sure that the placement of the mountain peak is at the same spot on each card so you have a consistent horizontal line across the entire piece.

Arrange the pieces from the background to the foreground, fuse in place, and trim any fabric overhanging the edges.

Cut 3 pieces of freezer paper 4" x 6". Trace the outline of the window and the mountain snowcap onto each piece. Mark the spring/fall snowmelt lines on two and the winter snowcap line on one.

Note that on the 4 windows there is more snow in winter, less in spring, an early dusting of snow in fall, and no snow in the summer.

Cut out the snowcap area with scissors and/or utility knife. If you cut down each side toward the downhill points of snow (where it collects in the valleys) you can get sharp points. If you cut a little too far, that is OK because when you iron the freezer paper to the window, those cuts will close up enough to prevent paint from seeping through.

Position the stencils over three of the mountain shapes and iron in place.

With a brush or sponge, daub white textile paint from the edges of the stencil into the center and use a pouncing motion to fill in the center area. For the fall window, lightly tap the brush on the lower edge of the stenciled area so that it looks like a dusting of newly fallen snow. Follow your paint manufacturer's instructions for setting or heat-setting the paint.

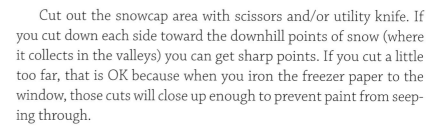

Allow the paint to set for a few moments but do not let it dry completely. Carefully peel the freezer paper off, lifting up from all edges towards the painted area/center. If the snow isn't as bright white as you like, let the first coat of paint dry, then add another coat before removing the stencil.

Cut 3" x 5" pieces from 3–4 pieces of branch fabric. Freeform cut slivers for the branches. Position on the windows and fuse in place.

For the spring window, cut cherry blossom petals and buds from two different pink fabrics. Position on the branches and fuse in place.

For the summer and fall windows, scrunch up some fabric and cut jaggedy-edged pieces for the clustered leaves. Position on the branches and fuse in place. Cut individual leaf shapes from assorted fabrics and fuse over the clusters.

Fuse backing onto the back of the windows. Trim the excess fabric.

Quilt each window leaving the skies unquilted. In selecting your thread, use lighter, brighter colors for the foreground and darker, more muted colors for the distant hills and mountain.

For the winter window, add a few clear glass beads to the branches to simulate ice.

Couch a thick yarn around the edges with Superior Bottom Line thread. You could also use a clear monofilament or silk that will disappear into the background. Try a regular zigzag, a three-step zigzag, or a decorative stitch such as a feather stitch for the couching.

Making the Background Quilt

Make a quilt sandwich from the background, batting, and backing. Position the windows on the quilt and draw a chalk line to connect the mountain peaks. Above that line, quilt cloud shapes. Below it, quilt hill shapes.

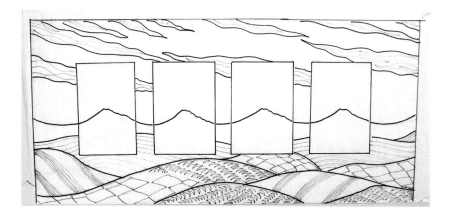

Sew 1" facing strips of fabric to match either the front or the backing to all 4 sides using a ¼" seam allowance. Press as sewn, then press the facings toward the seam allowance. Topstitch about ¹⁄₁₆" from the seam line in the seam allowance; this will encourage the seam allowance to stay put and not curl toward the front. Do not turn or sew the facings down yet.

Putting the Windows on the Background Quilt

Sew the windows to the background quilt by hand or machine. (I stitched by machine between the couched yarn and window using the same color thread I used for the couching.)

Press under ¼" on the raw edge of the facings, turn, and hand sew to the back of the quilt.

Prepare a hanging sleeve and stitch to the back.

Sign your piece on the back or on the front. (You're an artist now, and that's what artists do!)

Have a cup of tea and some chocolate and enjoy your artwork!

Options: *Make one window and use it as a decoration on a tote or a notebook cover. I adapted the spring window and used it on this tote bag, made with the Lazy Girl Designs Gracie tote bag pattern.*

Pattern displayed with the permission of Joan Hawley, Lazy Girl Designs, **www.lazygirldesigns.com**.

Metallic Threads & Stenciled Leaves

15" x 15", made by the author

TECHNIQUES: *stenciling, using metallic threads*

Fabrics and Notions

- 15" x 15" solid black cotton
- 19" x 19" cotton backing
- 19" x 19" batting
- 2 yards black chenille or cotton yarn (for couched yarn edge finish)
- Freezer paper square 15" x 15"
- Stencil brushes or paintbrushes
- Jacquard Lumiere paints in gold, silver, metallic green, and teal
- Threads for the top:
  Superior Metallics™ gold
  Superior Metallics variegated gold
  Superior Glitter™ gold
  Superior Glitter Pearl
  Superior Bottom Line™ black
  Superior 40-wt. polyester, pale blue
  Superior 40-wt polyester, variegated blue
- Threads for the bobbin:
  Superior Bottom Line black, pale gray, golden yellow, and medium blue

How-To

To make a stencil, transfer the pattern to the matte side of the freezer-paper square. Refer to the photograph (page 103) for placement and distribution.

Carefully cut out the leaf shapes and set them aside.

Iron the freezer-paper stencil onto the right side of the black cotton background.

Stencil the leaves.

Allow the paint to dry just a bit before removing the freezer paper.

Use the cut-out leaf shapes to trace around for leaves to simply outline with quilting.

Allow the paint to cure completely and set according to paint manufacturer's instructions.

Layer your quilt top with the batting and backing. Pin baste, being careful NOT to pin through the paint!

Although I would normally choose a size 14 Topstitch needle for sewing with metallic and Glitter threads, since the holes in painted fabric don't close up the way regular needle holes do, I would recommend a size 12 Topstitch needle.

Sew slowly. If your thread breaks, try again, starting the new stitching in the last hole made before the thread broke. If the thread breaks repeatedly, then go up a size to a 14 Topstitch needle. If you need to rip out and redo any stitching, use a very fine, small paintbrush to add just a teeny, tiny tip of paint to cover any holes.

Machine quilt the leaves, referring to the photographs on pages 103–104 for color placement. (I filled in the background with leaf shapes using some of the colored threads; I used Pearl Glitter for the wavy lines and fine black thread for the more tightly packed wavy pattern.)

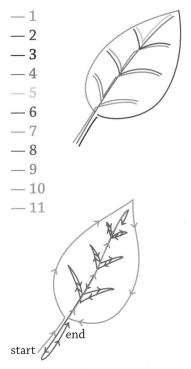

— 1
— 2
— 3
— 4
— 5
— 6
— 7
— 8
— 9
— 10
— 11

start end

Diagram of stitching sequences for a leaf

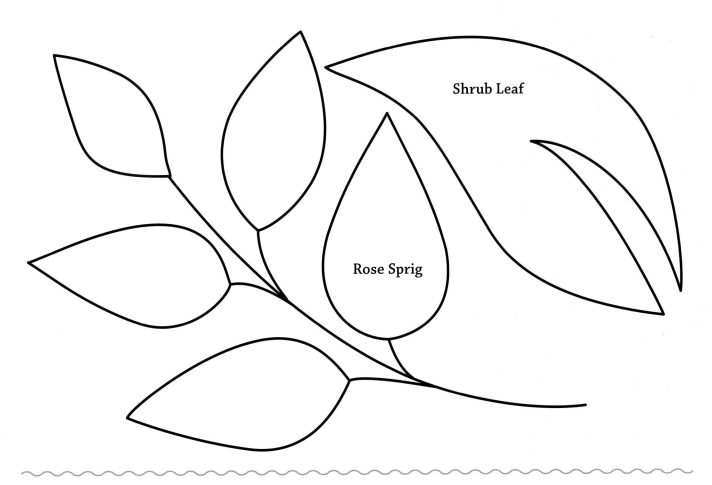

Shrub Leaf

Rose Sprig

Tossed Leaf Sampler

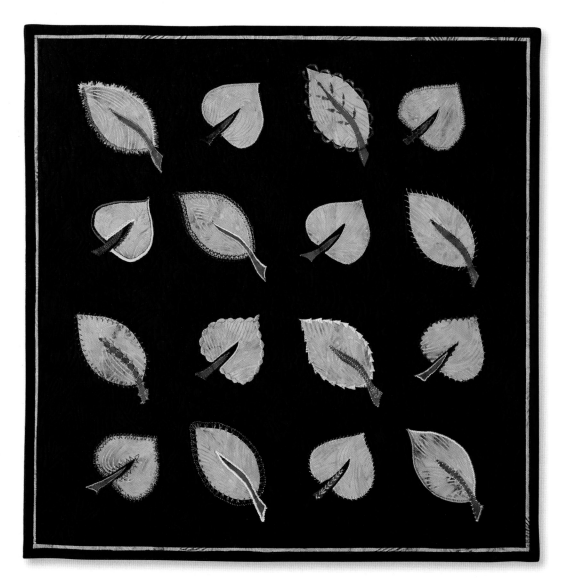

20" x 20", made by the author

TECHNIQUES: *fusible appliqué, decorative stitching*

Thanks to Jane Sassaman for the inspiration of her leaf sampler and for graciously agreeing to letting me use this one here!

My variation shows that even though using the same two fabrics, the leaves can look completely different just by changing the programmed stitch and thread color.

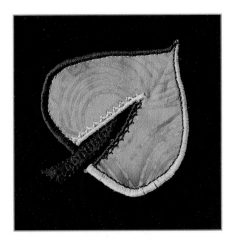

Fabrics and Notions

- 21" x 21" square background
- ¼ yard bright green for leaves, scraps of plum for stems
- ⅛ yard bright green cut into 4 strips 1" x 22" for accent border
- ¼ yard binding
- 25" x 25" batting and backing fabric
- assorted appliqué threads to match, coordinate with, and accent the fabrics
- ⅛ yard fusible web
- ¼ yard stabilizer—iron-on or tear-away
- appliqué pressing sheet or parchment paper to protect ironing board

Making the Sampler

Apply fusible web to the backs of the leaf and stem fabrics following the manufacturer's instructions.

Prepare a freezer paper template of the two leaf shapes (page 108).

Cut 8 each of the two leaf shapes and the two stems.

Position the leaves and stems on the background as shown or in your own arrangement, alternating the leaf shapes. Fuse in place.

Appliqué the leaves and stems in place with a variety of your machine's decorative stitches. Use stabilizer beneath the project and remove it when the stitching is complete.

I used freezer-paper for this project. I selected the upper right side for my light source. On some leaves, I used two shades of thread; by having the thread darker on one side of the leaf, it implies a shadow. The stitches I used are in the chart on page 108.

Layer the top with batting and backing. Secure for quilting by pin or spray basting.

There are many ways you can quilt your wall-hanging. I drew long, slightly curving lines horizontally and vertically across the top (like a jumbo tic-tac-toe). In each section I used a different fill pattern from my Nearly No-Mark Free-Motion Quilting Sampler (pages 93–94).

Trim the completed top to measure 20" x 20".

Accent, Binding, and Finishing

One at a time, place an accent strip (green in my quilt) even with the edge of the quilt and sew ½" from the outside edge.

Press the strip to the outside edge and trim it even with the quilt top edge. Baste in place using a 4.0 stitch length about ⅛" from the cut edge. Repeat along the remaining 3 sides.

Cut 2 straight-grain strips 1⅝" wide and join with a diagonal seam. Stitch the binding to the top using a ⅜" seam allowance, turn to the back, turn under the edge, and hand stitch in place.

Top left	LEAF AND STEM STITCHING		Top right
Grass stitch, two shades of green, outlined with a single straight stitch stem: ultra narrow satin stitch	**Zigzag,** 2.5 wide, 2.0 long, light and dark sides stem: zigzag, 2.0 wide, 1.5 long, light and dark sides	**Scallop stitch** in variegated thread stem: straight stitch	**Shorter grass stitch** and narrow satin stitch outlined with triple straight stitch stem: blind-hem stitch
Tapered satin stitch, outlined in opposite color, plus "V" along the center stem: decorative stitch down the center, triple straight stitch outline	**Decorative stitch** in medium and dark purple stem: statin stitch in light and medium purple	**Plain zigzag,** one color stem: the same	**Overcast stitch,** mirror-image in light color stem: stretch blind-hem stitch
Ornate feather stitch in contrasting color stem: diamond-shaped satin stitch	**Football shaped satin stitch** plus tapered satin stitch in contrasting color stem: blanket stitch	**Long triangles,** light and dark stem: decorative stitch down the center outlined with triple stretch stitch	**Small diamond satin stitch** in contrasting color stem: ulta tiny satin stitch
Decorative triangle in variegated thread stem: satin stitch	**Papyrus decorative stitch** in matching color stem: outlined satin stitch	**Simple faggoting or feather stitch** in light color stem: decorative leaf pattern down the center	**Satin stitch,** oulined in two color stem: faggoting stitch

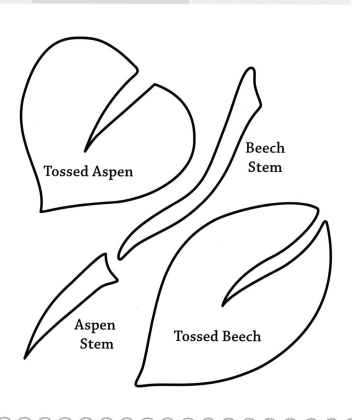

Tossed Aspen

Beech Stem

Aspen Stem

Tossed Beech

Resources

From Sarah's Bookshelf
An annotated bibliography and an annotated Resources list are available as free downloads from Sarah's blog. Go to:
www.sarahannsmith.com/weblog
In the left column click on downloads, then select the one(s) you wish.

Design Alternatives
Terry Hire's sewing machine table plans
100 Bayside Road
Northport, Maine 04843
alternatives@gwi.net

Dharma Trading Company
For dyes, paints, and PFD (prepared for dyeing) fabric
www.dharmatrading.com

Dick Blick Art Supplies
Online art supply store; find acetate sheets here
www.dickblick.com

Dyed and Gone to Heaven
Hand-dyed fabrics and patterns from
Lisa Walton, Sydney, Australia
www.dyedheaven.com

eQuilter
Online quilt shop
www.equilter.com

Superior Threads
Thread and great educational information. **www.superiorthreads.com**

Lazy Girl Designs
Many patterns including the Gracie bag pictured in the Mt. Fuji Seasons project.
www.lazygirldesigns.com

LaPierre Studio /
Free-Motion Slider
www.freemotionslider.com

Machine Quilting Unlimited
Fabulous magazine for all things machine quilty
www.mqumag.com

Misty Fuse
Home of Misty Fuse™ fusible webs and Transdoodle™ transfer paper
www.mistyfuse.com

The Pacific Rim Quilt Company
Sisters Nancy Lee Chong and Janice Lee Baehr designed their line and Web-site as a one-stop resource for Hawaiian quilting.
www.prqc.com or
www.pacificrimquiltco.com

ProChem
A complete range of Procion® MX dyes, PFD fabric, and a wide range of "How to" sheets available for download
www.prochemical.com

QuiltArt e-list
The best cyber-home for art quilters on the Internet. Visit them to find out how to join the ListServ and visit the Links page for loads of links to art quilters' sites. **www.quiltart.com**

TO MAKE THIS BOOK LIE FLAT
A "big-box" office supply store can cut off the spine and turn this into a spiral-bound book for about $5.

AND YOU CAN FIND ME HERE:
www.sarahannsmith.com

A NOTE TO QUILT TEACHERS:
This book is based on the classes I teach. If you'd like to know more about how to use this book to teach your own students, please contact me at **sarah@sarahannsmith.com** for free teaching information.

Thanks to the talented artists and businesspeople who generously shared their work and knowledge in this book. They have enriched the book, my quilting and I hope yours, too! Please visit them online:

Deirdre Abbotts
www.deirdreabbotts.com
Pamela Allen
www.pamelart.homestead.com
Deborah Boschert
www.deborahsStudio.com
Hollis Chatelain
www.hollisart.com
Kathy Daniels
www.studiointhewoods.blogspot.com
Gloria Hansen
www.gloriahansen.com
Joan Hawley
www.lazygirldesigns.com
Pat LaPierre
www.freemotionslider.com
Rana O'Connor
http://ranaquilts.blogspot.com
Bob Purcell
www.superiorthreads.com
Jane Sassaman
www.janesaman.com
Cindy Sissler Simms
www.cindysimms.net

Index

Meet Sarah Ann Smith

As a very young child Sarah lived in Spain, Thailand, and Argentina as her father, a former diplomat, traveled while working for an oil company. Shortly after her sixth birthday, her family returned to the United States to live. It was then that a neighbor girl made an apron for Sarah's favorite doll, sparking a fascination with textiles and fiber that continues to this day. Her only problem is that no one has yet created a 37-hour day!

While she was working at the U.S. embassy in La Paz, Bolivia, Sarah came across someone's discarded Keepsake Quilting catalog, which opened up the doors to the quilting world. She hasn't looked back since. Sarah's work has been juried into shows and published in magazines and books in the U.S. and Europe, and is in public and private collections including the International Quilt Festival Collection. A former U.S. Foreign Service officer, she draws on her assignments in Africa, South America, and North America, as well as travels to Asia and Europe, as inspiration for her art.

Sarah specializes in machine work, coloring with threads, and using whatever technique will help turn the picture in her mind into cloth. She is a full-time artist, member of the Frayed Edges mini-group, quilt teacher, and pattern designer. Sarah lives in Camden, Maine, with her husband, two sons, a pug, four cats, and assorted dust bunnies and relishes her supportive environment for textile art and art quilts. She has learned that if you want to, and are willing to work at it, you can make your dreams come true.

To see more of Sarah's art, her teaching schedule and blog, or to contact her, visit **www.sarahannsmith.com** and **www.sarahannsmith.com/weblog**.

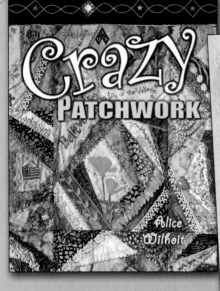